Human Rights And International Law Practice

HUMAN RIGHTS AND INTERNATIONAL LAW PRACTICE

A N Dange

MD PUBLICATIONS PVT LTD
NEW DELHI
www.mdppl.com

Published by :

MD Publications Pvt Ltd
"MD House", 11, Darya Ganj,
New Delhi - 110 002
Phone : +91-11- 45355555
E-mail : contact@mdppl.com
Website: www.mdppl.com

ISBN : 978-81-7533-342-0

Published and Printed by Mr. Pranav Gupta on behalf of **MD Publications Pvt Ltd** at Repro India Limited.

Preface

International human rights law refers to the body of international law designed to promote and protect human rights at the international, regional and domestic levels. As a form of international law, international human rights law is primarily made up of treaties, agreements between states intended to have binding legal effect between the parties that have agreed to them; and customary international law, rules of law derived from the consistent conduct of states acting out of the belief that the law required them to act that way. Other international human rights instruments while not legally binding contribute to the implementation, understanding and development of international human rights law and have been recognized as a source of political obligation. The enforcement of international human rights law can occur on either a domestic, regional or international level. States that ratify human rights treaties commit themselves to respecting those rights and ensuring that their domestic law is compatible with international legislation.

International Human rights law is closely related to, but distinct from international humanitarian law. Similar, because the substantive norms they contain are often similar or related for example both provide a protection from torture. Distinct because they are regulated by legally distinct frameworks and usually operate in different contexts and regulate different relationships. Generally, human rights are understood to regulate the relationship between states and individuals in the context of ordinary life.

This book is an attempt to analyse the relationship between International Law and Human Rights and demonstrate the impact international law has had on International level. The impact of international law upon Human Rights has been considerable, especially in the area of global world; thus, the primary focus is placed upon issues of human rights.

The International Covenant on Economic, Social and Cultural Rights and the International Covenant on Civil and Political Rights came into force in 1976. Though I dealt with treaties in general in the book, the focus of my concern was treaties on human rights. And, while the conclusions drawn in the book should be valid not only in one country but also in other countries. The present book, which deals specifically with developments in World in the area of human rights. I am grateful to all those who were kind enough to read various parts of the draft manuscript at different stages and comment upon them. I also thank my friends and colleagues for their technical assistance. My special thanks my parents and for my family for their understanding and support.

I am very grateful to Mr. Pranav Gupta, Director of MD Publications Pvt Ltd, New Delhi, for his kind cooperation and support for this book.

A N Dange

CONTENTS

1

Human Rights and International Law

Introduction

International human rights law refers to the body of International Law designed to promote & protect human rights at the international, regional and domestic levels. International Human Rights Law is primarily made up of International Treaties & Customary International Law. However, other international human rights instruments in the form of Declarations, Guidelines and International Principles contribute to the implementation, understanding and development of international human rights law.

International Human Rights Law can be enforced on either a Domestic, Regional or International Level. States that ratify human rights treaties commit themselves to respecting those rights and ensuring that their domestic law is compatible with their international legislation. Customary peremptory norms of International Law that relate to human rights are considered binding on all nations, although the status of such norms is commonly disputed.

When Domestic Law fails to provide a remedy for human rights abuses parties may be able to resort to regional or international mechanisms for enforcing human rights.

International Human Rights Law is related to, but not the same as International Humanitarian Law, which regulates armed conflicts and Refugee Law. War crimes, crimes against humanity and genocide may be regulated by international human rights law but each have a substantial body of independent international law.

The Universal Declaration of Human Rights (UDHR) is a declaration adopted by the United Nations General Assembly on 10 December, 1948 at the Palais de Chaillot in Paris. The Declaration has been translated into at least 375 languages and dialects, making it the most widely translated document in the world. The Declaration arose directly from the experience of the Second World War and represents the first global expression of rights to which all human beings are entitled. It consists of 30 articles which have been elaborated in subsequent international treaties, regional human rights instruments, national constitutions and laws. The International Bill of Human Rights consists of the Universal Declaration of Human Rights, the International Covenant on Economic, Social and Cultural Rights, and the International Covenant on Civil and Political Rights and its two Optional Protocols. In 1966, the General Assembly adopted the two detailed Covenants, which complete the International Bill of Human Rights.

History

Conception – The morals and values of human rights can be traced through the history of religious beliefs and cultures around the world. European philosophers of the Age of Enlightenment developed theories of natural law that influenced the adoption of documents such as the Bill of Rights of England, the Bill of Rights in the United States, and the

Declaration of the Rights of Man and of the Citizen in France.

National and International pressure for an international bill of rights had been building throughout World War II. In his 1941 State of the Union address US president Franklin Roosevelt called for the protection of what he termed the "essential" Four Freedoms: freedom of speech, freedom of conscience, freedom from fear and freedom from want, as its basic war aims. This has been seen as part of a movement of the 1940s that sought to make human rights part of the conditions for peace at the end of the war. The United Nations Charter "reaffirmed faith in fundamental human rights, and dignity and worth of the human person" and committed all member states to promote "universal respect for, and observance of, human rights and fundamental freedoms for all without distinction as to race, sex, language or religion".

When the atrocities committed by Nazi Germany became public knowledge around the world after World War II, the consensus within the world community was that the United Nations Charter did not sufficiently define the rights it referenced. A universal declaration that specified the rights of individuals was necessary to give effect to the Charter's provisions on human rights.

Drafting – Canadian John Peters Humphrey was called upon by the United Nations Secretary-General to work on the project and became the Declaration's principal drafter. At the time Humphrey was newly appointed as Director of the Division of Human Rights within the United Nations Secretariat. The Commission on Human Rights, a standing body of the United Nations, was constituted to undertake the work of preparing what was initially conceived as an International Bill of Rights. The membership of the Commission was designed to be broadly representative of the global community with representatives of the following countries serving: Australia, Belgium, Byelorussian Soviet Socialist Republic, Chile, China, Cuba, Egypt, France, India, Iran, Lebanon, Panama, Philippines, United Kingdom, United States, Soviet Union, Uruguay and Yugoslavia.

Adoption – The Universal Declaration was adopted by the General Assembly on 10 December, 1948 by a vote of 48 in favour, 0 against, with 8 abstentions (Byelorussian SSR, Czechoslovakia, Poland, Ukrainian SSR, USSR, as well as Yugoslavia, South Africa and Saudi Arabia).

The following countries voted in favour of the Declaration: Afghanistan, Argentina, Australia, Belgium, Bolivia, Brazil, Burma, Canada, Chile, China, Colombia, Costa Rica, Cuba, Denmark, the Dominican Republic, Ecuador, Egypt, El Salvador, Ethiopia, France, Greece, Guatemala, Haiti, Iceland, India, Iran, Iraq, Lebanon, Liberia, Luxembourg, Mexico, Netherlands, New Zealand, Nicaragua, Norway, Pakistan, Panama, Paraguay, Peru, Philippines, Thailand, Sweden, Syria, Turkey, United Kingdom, United States, Uruguay and Venezuela.

Despite the central role played by Canadian John Humphrey, the Canadian Government at first abstained from voting on the Declaration's draft, but later voted in favour of the final draft in the General Assembly.

Structure

The underlying structure of the Universal Declaration was introduced in its second draft which was prepared by Rene Cassin. Cassin worked from a first draft prepared by John Peters Humphrey. The structure was influenced by the Code Napoleon, including a preamble and introductory general principles. Cassin compared the Declaration to the portico of a Greek temple, with a foundation, steps, four columns and a pediment. Articles 1 and 2 are the foundation blocks, with their principles of dignity, liberty, equality and brotherhood. The seven paragraphs of the preamble, setting out the reasons for the Declaration, are represented by the steps. The main body of the Declaration forms the four columns. The first column (articles 3–11) constitutes rights of the individual, such as the right to life and the prohibition of slavery. The second column (articles 12–17) constitutes the rights of the individual in civil and political society. The third column (articles 18–21) is concerned with spiritual, public and political freedoms such as freedom of religion and freedom of association. The fourth column (articles 22–27) sets out social, economic and cultural rights. In Cassin's model, the last three articles of the Declaration provide the pediment which binds the structure together. These articles are concerned with the duty of the individual to society and the prohibition of use of rights in contravention of the purposes of the United Nations. With regard to the Communist block's abstentions, the 9 December Velodrome d'Hiver meeting of 20,000 Parisiens at the invitation of World Citizen Garry Davis and his "Conseil de Solidarité" who had interrupted a General Assembly session on 22 November to call for a world government, provoked its abstention rather than voting against the human rights document. Eleanor Roosevelt in her column "My Day" wrote on 15 December that "Garry Davis, the young man who in Paris as a citizen of the world has succeeded in getting the backing of a few intellectuals and even has received a cablegram from Albert Einstein telling him, from Professor Einstein's point of view, that the United Nations has not yet achieved peace. The United Nations, of course, is not set up to achieve peace. That the governments are supposed to do themselves. But it is expected to help preserve peace, and that I think, is it doing more effectively day by day. During a pleneary session in the General Assembly, this young man tried to make a speech from the balcony on the subject of how incompetent the United Nations is to deal with the questions before it. How much better it would be if Mr. Davis would set up his own governmental organisation and start then and there a worldwide international government. All who would join him would learn that they had no nationality and, therefore, not being bothered by any special interest in any one country, everyone would develop a completely cooperative feeling among all peoples and a willingness to accept any laws passes by this super government."

Preamble

The Universal Declaration begins with a preamble consisting of seven paragraphs followed by a statement "proclaiming" the Declaration.

Each paragraph of the preamble sets out a reason for the adoption of the Declaration. The first paragraph asserts that the recognition of human dignity of all people is the foundation of justice and peace in the world. The second paragraph observes that disregard and contempt for human rights have resulted in barbarous acts which have outraged the conscience of mankind and that the four freedoms: freedom of speech, belief, freedom from want, and freedom from fear which is "proclaimed as the highest aspiration" of the people. The third paragraph states that so that people are not compelled to rebellion against tyranny, human rights should be protected by rule of law. The fourth paragraph relates human rights to the development of friendly relations between nations. The fifth paragraph links the Declaration back to the United Nations Charter which reaffirms faith in fundamental human rights and dignity and worth of the human person. The sixth paragraph notes that all members of the United Nations have pledged themselves to achieve, in cooperation with the United Nations, the promotion of universal respect for and observance of human rights and fundamental freedoms. The seventh paragraph observes that "a common understanding" of rights and freedoms is of "the greatest importance" for the full realisation of that pledge.

These paragraphs are followed by the "proclamation" of the Declaration as a "common standard of achievement" for "all peoples and all nations", so that "all individuals" and "all organs of society" should by teaching and education, promote respect for these rights and freedoms and by progressive measures, national and international, secure their universal and effective recognition and observance.

The Preamble is:

- **Whereas** recognition of the inherent dignity and of

the equal and inalienable rights of all members of the human family is the foundation of freedom, justice and peace in the world,

- **Whereas** disregard and contempt for human rights have resulted in barbarous acts which have outraged the conscience of mankind, and the advent of a world in which human beings shall enjoy freedom of speech and belief and freedom from fear and want has been proclaimed as the highest aspiration of the common people,
- **Whereas** it is essential, if man is not to be compelled to have recourse, as a last resort, to rebellion against tyranny and oppression, that human rights should be protected by the rule of law,
- **Whereas** it is essential to promote the development of friendly relations between nations,
- **Whereas** the peoples of the United Nations have in the Charter reaffirmed their faith in fundamental human rights, in the dignity and worth of the human person and in the equal rights of men and women and have determined to promote social progress and better standards of life in larger freedom,
- **Whereas** Member States have pledged themselves to achieve, in co-operation with the United Nations, the promotion of universal respect for and observance of human rights and fundamental freedoms,
- **Whereas** a common understanding of these rights and freedoms is of the greatest importance for the full realization of this pledge,
- **Now, Therefore** THE GENERAL ASSEMBLY proclaims THIS UNIVERSAL DECLARATION OF HUMAN RIGHTS as a common standard of achievement for all peoples and all nations, to the end that every individual and every organ of society, keeping this Declaration constantly in mind, shall strive by teaching and education to promote respect for these rights and freedoms and by progressive measures, national and

international, to secure their universal and effective recognition and observance, both among the peoples of Member States themselves and among the peoples of territories under their jurisdiction.

Human Rights Set Out in the Declaration

The following reproduces the articles of the Declaration which set out the specific human rights that are recognised in the Declaration.

Article 1 : All human beings are born free and equal in dignity and rights. They are endowed with reason and conscience and should act towards one another in a spirit of brotherhood.

Article 2 : Everyone is entitled to all the rights and freedoms set forth in this Declaration, without distinction of any kind, such as race, colour, sex, language, religion, political or other opinion, national or social origin, property, birth or other status. Furthermore, no distinction shall be made on the basis of the political, jurisdictional or international status of the country or territory to which a person belongs, whether it be independent, trust, non-self-governing or under any other limitation of sovereignty.

Article 3 : Everyone has the right to life, liberty and security of person.

Article 4 : No one shall be held in slavery or servitude; slavery and the *slave trade* shall be prohibited in all their forms.

Article 5 : No one shall be subjected to torture or to cruel, inhuman or degrading treatment or punishment.

Article 6 : Everyone has the right to recognition everywhere as a person before the law.

Article 7 : All are equal before the law and are entitled without any discrimination to equal protection of the law. All are entitled to equal protection against any discrimination in violation of this Declaration and against any incitement to such discrimination.

Article 8 : Everyone has the right to an effective remedy by the competent national tribunals for acts violating *the fundamental rights* granted him by the constitution or by law.

Article 9 : No one shall be subjected to arbitrary arrest, detention or exile.

Article 10 : Everyone is entitled in full equality to a fair and public hearing by an independent and impartial tribunal, in the determination of his rights and obligations and of any criminal charge against him.

Article 11

1. Everyone charged with a penal offence has the right to be presumed innocent until proved guilty according to law in a public trial at which he has had all the guarantees necessary for his defence.
2. No one shall be held guilty of any penal offence on account of any act or omission which did not constitute a penal offence, under national or international law, at the time when it was committed. Nor shall a heavier penalty be imposed than the one that was applicable at the time the penal offence was committed.

Article 12 : No one shall be subjected to arbitrary interference with his privacy, family, home or correspondence, nor to attacks upon his honour and reputation. Everyone has the right to the protection of the law against such interference or attacks.

Article 13

1. Everyone has the right to freedom of movement and residence within the borders of each state.
2. Everyone has the right to leave any country, including their own, and to return to their country.

Article 14

1. Everyone has the right to seek and to enjoy in other countries *asylum from* persecution.
2. This right may not be invoked in the case of

prosecutions genuinely arising from non-political crimes or from acts contrary to the purposes and principles of the United Nations.

Article 15

1. Everyone has the right to a nationality.
2. No one shall be arbitrarily deprived of his nationality nor denied the right to change his nationality.

Article 16

1. Men and women of full age, without any limitation due to race, nationality or religion, have the right to marry and to found a family. They are entitled to equal rights as to marriage, during marriage and at its dissolution.
2. Marriage shall be entered into only with the free and full consent of the intending spouses.
3. The family is the natural and fundamental group unit of society and is entitled to protection by society and the State.

Article 17

1. Everyone has the right to own property alone as well as in association with others.
2. No one shall be arbitrarily deprived of his property.

Article 18 : Everyone has the right to freedom of thought, *conscience* and religion; this right includes freedom to change his religion or belief, and freedom, either alone or in community with others and in public or private, to manifest his religion or belief in teaching, practice, worship and observance.

Article 19 : Everyone has the right to freedom of opinion and expression; this right includes freedom to hold opinions without interference and to seek, receive and impart information and ideas through any media and regardless of frontiers.

Article 20

1. Everyone has the right to freedom of peaceful assembly and association.

2. No one may be compelled to belong to an association.

Article 21

1. Everyone has the right to take part in the government of their country, directly or through freely chosen representatives.
2. Everyone has the right of equal access to public service in their country.
3. The will of the people shall be the basis of the authority of government; this will shall be expressed in periodic and genuine elections which shall be by universal and equal suffrage and shall be held by secret vote or by equivalent free voting procedures.

Article 22 : Everyone, as a member of society, has the right to social security and is entitled to realization, through national effort and international co-operation and in accordance with the organisation and resources of each State, of the economic, social and cultural rights indispensable for his dignity and the free development of his personality.

Article 23

1. Everyone has the right to work, to free choice of employment, to just and favourable conditions of work and to protection against unemployment.
2. Everyone, without any discrimination, has the right to equal pay for equal work.
3. Everyone who works has the right to just and favourable remuneration ensuring for himself and his family an existence worthy of human dignity, and supplemented, if necessary, by other means of social protection.
4. Everyone has the right to form and to join trade unions for the protection of his interests.

Article 24 : Everyone has the right to rest and leisure, including reasonable limitation of working hours and periodic holidays with pay.

Article 25

1. Everyone has the right to a standard of living adequate for the health and well-being of himself and of his family, including food, clothing, housing and medical care and necessary social services, and the right to security in the event of unemployment, sickness, disability, widowhood, old age or other lack of livelihood in circumstances beyond his control.
2. Motherhood and childhood are entitled to special care and assistance. All children, whether born in or *out of wedlock*, shall enjoy the same social protection.

Article 26

1. Everyone has the right to education. Education shall be free, at least in the elementary and fundamental stages. Elementary education shall be compulsory. Technical and professional education shall be made generally available and higher education shall be equally accessible to all on the basis of merit.
2. Education shall be directed to the full development of the human personality and to the strengthening of respect for human rights and fundamental freedoms. It shall promote understanding, tolerance and friendship among all nations, racial or religious groups, and shall further the activities of the United Nations for the maintenance of peace.
3. Parents have a prior right to choose the kind of education that shall be given to their children.

Article 27

1. Everyone has the right freely to participate in the cultural life of the community, to enjoy the arts and to share in scientific advancement and its benefits.
2. Everyone has the right to the protection of the moral and material interests resulting from any scientific, literary or artistic production of which he is the author.

Article 28 : Everyone is entitled to a social and international order in which the rights and freedoms set forth in this Declaration can be fully realised.

Article 29

1. Everyone has duties to the community in which alone the free and full development of his personality is possible.
2. In the exercise of his rights and freedoms, everyone shall be subject only to such limitations as are determined by law solely for the purpose of securing due recognition and respect for the rights and freedoms of others and of meeting the just requirements of morality, public order and the general welfare in a democratic society.
3. These rights and freedoms may in no case be exercised contrary to the purposes and principles of the United Nations.

Article 30 : Nothing in this Declaration may be interpreted as implying for any State, group or person any right to engage in any activity or to perform any act aimed at the destruction of any of the rights and freedoms set forth herein.

Commemoration: International Human Rights Day

The adoption of the Universal Declaration is a significant international commemoration marked each year on 10 December and is known as Human Rights Day or International Human Rights Day. The commemoration is observed by individuals, community and religious groups, human rights organisations, parliaments, governments and the United Nations. Decadal commemorations are often accompanied by campaigns to promote awareness of the Declaration and human rights, 2008 marked the 60th anniversary of the Declaration and was accompanied by year long activities around the theme "Dignity and justice for all of us".

Significance and Legal Effect

Significance – In the preamble, governments commit themselves and their peoples to measures to secure the universal and effective recognition and observance of the human rights set out in the Declaration. Eleanor Roosevelt supported the adoption the UDHR as a declaration, rather than as a treaty, because she believed that it would have the same kind of influence on global society as the United States Declaration of Independence had within the United States. In this she proved to be correct. Even though not formally legally binding, the Declaration has been adopted in or influenced most national constitutions since 1948. It also serves as the foundation for a growing number of international treaties and national laws and international, regional, national and sub-national institutions protecting and promoting human rights.

Legal effect – While not a treaty itself, the Declaration was explicitly adopted for the purpose of defining the meaning of the words "fundamental freedoms" and "human rights" appearing in the United Nations Charter, which is binding on all member states. For this reason, the Universal Declaration is a fundamental constitutive document of the United Nations. Many international lawyers, in addition, believe that the Declaration forms part of customary international law and is a powerful tool in applying diplomatic and moral pressure to governments that violate any of its articles. The 1968 United Nations International Conference on Human Rights advised that it "constitutes an obligation for the members of the international community" to all persons. The Declaration has served as the foundation for two binding UN human rights covenants, the International Covenant on Civil and Political Rights and the International Covenant on Economic, Social and Cultural Rights and the principles of the Declaration are elaborated in international treaties such as the International Convention on the Elimination of All Forms of Racial Discrimination, the International Convention on the Elimination of Discrimination Against Women, the United Nations Convention on the Rights of the Child, the United Nations Convention Against Torture and many more. The Declaration continues to be widely cited by governments, academics, advocates and constitutional courts and individual human beings who appeal to its principles for the protection of their recognised human rights.

Reaction

Praise – The Universal Declaration has received praise from a number of notable people. Charles Malik, Lebanese philosopher and diplomat, called it "an international document of the first order of importance," while Eleanor Roosevelt, first chairwoman of the Commission on Human Rights (CHR) that drafted the Declaration, stated that it "may well become the international Magna Carta of all men everywhere," 10 December, 1948. In a speech on 5 October 1995, Pope John Paul II called the UDHR "one of the highest expressions of the human conscience of our time." And in a statement on 10 December, 2003 on behalf of the European Union, Marcello Spatafora said that "it placed human rights at the centre of the framework of principles and obligations shaping relations within the international community."

Criticism

Islamic criticism – Some Islamic countries have criticised the Universal Declaration of Human Rights for its perceived failure to take into the account the cultural and religious context of Islamic countries. In 1982, the Iranian representative to the United Nations, Said Rajaie-Khorassani, articulated the position of his country regarding the Universal Declaration of Human Rights, by saying that the UDHR was "a secular understanding of the Judeo-Christian tradition", which could not be implemented by Muslims without trespassing the Islamic law. On 30 June, 2000, Muslim nations that are members of the Organization of the Islamic Conference officially resolved to support the Cairo Declaration on Human Rights in Islam, an alternative document that says people have "freedom and right to a dignified life in accordance with the Islamic Shari'ah". However, this document does not guarantee freedom of religion or gender equality, the root of many criticisms against its usage.

Education – Some proponents of alternative education, particularly unschooling, take issue with the right to compulsory education stated in Article 26. In the philosophies of John Holt and others, compulsory education itself violates the right of a person to follow their own interests:

No human right, except the right to life itself, is more fundamental than this. A person's freedom of learning is part of his freedom of thought, even more basic than his freedom of speech. If we take from someone his right to decide what he will be curious about, we destroy his freedom of thought. We say, in effect, you must think not about what interests you and concerns you, but about what interests and concerns us.

Property Rights Criticism – Some Libertarians have criticised the Declaration for its inclusion of positive rights that they believe must be provided by others through forceful extraction thereby negating others rights. Libertarian natural law theorist Frank Van Dun said of the document:

> *The UD's distinctive "rights" are incompatible with that doctrine [of natural rights]. Enforcement of one person's economic, social, or cultural rights necessarily involves forcing others to relinquish their property, or to use it in a way prescribed by the enforcers. It would, therefore, constitute a clear violation of their natural right to manage and dispose of their lawful possessions without coercive or aggressive interference by others. It would also deny a person the right to improve his condition by accepting work for what he (but perhaps no one else) considers an adequate wage.*

The Right to Refuse to Kill – Groups such as Amnesty International and War Resisters International have advocated for "The Right to Refuse to Kill" to be added to the UDHR. War Resisters International has stated that the right to conscientious objection to military service is primarily derived from, but not yet explicit in, Article 18 of the UDHR: the right to freedom of thought, conscience and religion.

Steps have been taken within the United Nations to make this right more explicit; but those steps have been limited to secondary, more "marginal" United Nations documents. That is why Amnesty International would like to have this right brought "out of the margins" and explicitly into the primary document, namely the UDHR itself.

To the rights enshrined in the Universal Declaration of Human Rights one more might, with relevance, be added. It is "The Right to Refuse to Kill."

Bangkok Declaration – In the Bangkok Declaration adopted by Ministers of Asian states meeting in 1993 in the lead up to the World Conference on Human Rights, Asian governments reaffirmed their commitment to the principles of the United Nations Charter and the Universal Declaration of Human Rights. They stated their view of the interdependence and indivisibility of human rights and stressed the need for universality, objectivity and non-selectivity of human rights.

Enforcement of Human Rights Law

There is currently no international court to administer international human rights law, however, quasi-judicial bodies exists under some UN treaties (e.g., Human Rights Committee under ICCPR). The International Criminal Court (ICC) has jurisdiction over the crime of genocide, war crimes and crimes against humanity. While the European Court of Human Rights, and the Inter-American Court of Human Rights enforce regional human rights law. Although these same international bodies also hold jurisdiction over cases regarding international humanitarian law, it is crucial to recognize that the two frameworks constitute distinctly different legal regimes.

The United Nations Human Rights Bodies do have some quasi legal enforcement mechanisms. These include the Treaty Bodies attached to the current seven active treaties, and the Human Rights Council complaints procedures, known as the 1235 and 1503 mechanisms.

In practice, many human rights are very difficult to legally enforce due to the absence of consensus on the application of certain rights, the lack of relevant national legislation or of bodies empowered to take legal action to enforce them.

In over 110 countries national human rights institutions (NHRIs) have been set up to protect, promote or monitor human rights with jurisdiction in a given country. Although not all NHRIs are compliant with the Paris Principles, the number and effect of these institutions is increasing. The Paris Principles were defined at the first International Workshop on National Institutions for the Promotion and Protection of Human Rights in Paris on 7-9 October 1991, and adopted by United Nations Human Rights Commission Resolution 1992/54 of 1992 and the General Assembly Resolution 48/134 of 1993. The Paris Principles list a number of responsibilities for national institutions.

Universal Jurisdiction

Universal jurisdiction is a controversial principle in international law whereby states claim criminal jurisdiction over persons whose alleged crimes were committed outside the boundaries of the prosecuting state, regardless of nationality, country of residence, or any other relation with the prosecuting country. The state backs its claim on the grounds that the crime committed is considered a crime against all, which any state is authorized to punish. The concept of universal jurisdiction is therefore closely linked to the idea that certain international norms are erga omnes, or owed to the entire world community, as well as the concept of jus cogens. In 1993 Belgium passed a *law of universal jurisdiction* to give its courts jurisdiction over crimes against humanity in other countries, and in 1998 Augusto Pinochet was arrested in London following an indictment by Spanish judge Baltasar Garzon under the universal jurisdiction principle. The principle is supported by Amnesty International and other human rights organisations as they believe certain crimes pose a threat to the international community as a whole and the community has a moral duty to act, but others, including Henry Kissinger argue that "widespread agreement that human rights violations and crimes against humanity must be prosecuted has hindered active consideration of the proper role of international courts.

2

Contemporary Issues and Human Rights Violations

Introduction

The complex nature of human rights protection and promotion, such as the debate over whom is entitled to receive asylum, the arguments made by proponents of female genital mutilation, the differing opinions on the age a child is old enough to fight a war, and the legal intricacies involved in extraditing criminals.

Through investigating contemporary human rights violations and the inspiring efforts to oppose them, it becomes clear that rights are interconnected, indivisible, and nonhierarchical. Human rights issues are not defined by the wealth or geography of a nation. Homelessness occurs worldwide, as does rape. While developed nations may have fewer landmines and refugees, and their citizens may enjoy greater political and press freedom than in developing countries, human rights are blind to nationality, ethnicity, gender, age, sexual orientation, or religion. Issues such as police brutality, self-determination, and discrimination based on sexual preference or HIV/AIDS status are of equal relevance in Uganda as they are in the United States. While respect for human rights varies from nation to nation and fluctuates over time, human rights shouldn't be left or picked up at any airport or border.

Human rights issues overlap. Militaries, including armed opposition groups, recruit child soldiers and mistreat prisoners. Rape can be a form of genocide. Human rights activists are served the death penalty, disappeared, detained, or executed for defending their rights and the rights of others. Children are subject to bonded labour, slavery, and trafficking. And when they are poor, homeless, displaced, or living with HIV/AIDS, children are even more vulnerable. Females young and old suffer gender-related abuses; in some nations they are afforded fewer political rights or denied access to health care, education, and freedom of movement.

Many of the human rights issues point to the disparity of wealth in a world that values cultural, social, and economic richness of all people's lives. Cultural rights, self-determination, indigenous rights, and the right to development are all related to the economic majority's lack of respect for the inherent rights and freedoms of indigenous peoples and linguistic, ethnic, and religious minorities.

What mitigates indignation about human rights abuses is recognition of the tireless work to raise awareness on the issues, to change policy and practices, and ultimately to stop the abuses. These pages recount the countless and often nameless individuals and organizations who promote and protect human rights. Child labour activists in Nepal, publishers in Vietnam, and civilian deminers in Angola work to defend human rights, and ultimately to protect human security often at their own personal risk.

The many individuals and groups around the world, with their steadfast endeavours to effect change, infuse vitality into human rights that to a great extent have existed primarily on paper. For example, the intergovernmental organization, the International Committee of the Red Cross, works to promote and protect the rights of prisoners, the detained, and it also defends medical neutrality. International nongovernmental organizations (NGOs) such as Human Rights Watch conduct systematic investigations of human rights abuses worldwide, holding governments accountable if they transgress human rights.

The United Nations on a wide variety of human rights questions, such 'as the drafting of a Declaration on Indigenous Rights and supporting efforts to form an International Criminal Court. The UN has appointed special *rapporteurs* on issues such as child soldiers, the independence of judges and lawyers, and torture. Specialized bodies such as UNICEF make pleas against female genital mutilation and the UN High Commission on Refugees works to deal with the world's massive refugee population. The initiatives surveyed in these entries cry for more support.

While the UN is sometimes criticized for ineffectiveness or for simply not doing enough, this chapter also demonstrates how often we look to it to stop human rights abuses. Without the political will of the world's nations that constitute the UN, its bodies cannot be agents of lasting change. The Universal Declaration of Human Rights (UDHR), while imperfect, is a revolutionary notion. The following essays show that human rights, as defined in the UDHR and a growing number of human rights declarations and treaties, are violated daily. But they also demonstrate the inextinguishable struggle for justice, freedom, human rights, and dignity.

AIDS/HIV

Human rights concerns surrounding acquired immunodeficiency syndrome (AIDS) are both political and medical. Discrimination based on actual or suspected infection with the human immunodeficiency virus (HIV) is an especially pressing concern. Other human rights standards important in the context of HIV/AIDS are education, including access to information about HIV; health, including the right to equal access to means of prevention of HIV; privacy, including the right to keep medical tests secret; and freedom from sexual exploitation and violence.

AIDS was first identified in 1981. Initially, little was known about how the disease spread, which resulted in people with AIDS (PWAs) often being the targets of fear and discrimination. It was subsequently discovered that AIDS spreads in a variety of ways, including unprotected sexual intercourse and the sharing of needles by intravenous drug users. In the industrialized world one of the populations most profoundly affected by the disease was homosexual men. Fear of AIDS has provided an excuse for homophobia and has fed into hate crimes and other human rights violations of homosexuals. Worldwide, nearly twelve million people have died from AIDS, and thirty million more are living with AIDS or HIV. Approximately ten million of these PWAs are between ten and twenty-four years old. Sixteen thousand people are newly infected with HIV every day. If no cure is found, the thirty million people who currently have HIV could be dead within ten years.

Discrimination based on actual or suspected HIV infection is a violation of international law norms. Despite this, in 1989 an HIV-positive Dutch citizen was denied entry into the United States to speak at an AIDS conference in San Francisco. Currently, PWAs are not allowed to immigrate into the United States, although the attorney general may waive that regulation if the person has family already in the United States. PWAs entering the United States to visit or attend conferences are no longer restricted. Often PWAs also suffer job and housing discrimination due to their illness, although this has been outlawed; in the United States, for example, it is covered under the 1990 Americans with Disabilities Act.

Each year doctors learn more about treating and preventing AIDS. Nonetheless, almost six million people were infected with HIV in 1997 alone. In 1996, for the first time, deaths from AIDS decreased in the United States, due to new treatment discoveries. This is not true in the rest of the world: two-thirds of AIDS deaths occur in sub-Saharan Africa and the number continues to rise. In Botswana and Zimbabwe one quarter of the adult population has AIDS; by the year 2005, 1.2 million adults in Zimbabwe will die from AIDS. In Malawi the average life expectancy prior to the AIDS epidemic was fifty-one; now it is thirty-seven. As a result of these adult deaths, there are now eight million orphans living in sub-Saharan Africa.

Although AIDS was at one time believed to be a "gay disease" or "drug addicts' disease," one segment of society that is particularly vulnerable to HIV today is young people: approximately one-third of people with AIDS are between ten and twenty-four years old. Pregnant teens are also at risk: in Zimbabwe 30 percent of pregnant fifteen-to nineteen-year-olds are HIV positive. Another group that is especially susceptible is young prostitutes. In some cases prostitutes' clients mistakenly believe that young girls cannot carry HIV and are therefore "safe." This contributes to the abduction of younger and younger girls for prostitution. Unfortunately, children are actually more vulnerable to AIDS than adults. In Uganda it is believed that prostitutes under the age of nineteen test HIV positive three times as often as adult prostitutes. In Cambodia 30 per cent of sex workers under nineteen are infected; in Thailand 50 per cent are HIV positive.

In 1996, the United Nations created UNAIDS, a joint venture of the United Nations Children's Fund, the United Nations Development Program, the United Nations Population Fund, and the United Nations Educational, Scientific, and Cultural Organization, along with the World Health Organization and the World Bank. The goals of UNAIDS are to coordinate action by many AIDS organizations, analyze information about AIDS to determine the best policies for prevention and treatment, advocate among various governments and non-governmental organizations to implement AIDS policies, and gather and examine information on the global AIDS epidemic. It is hoped this will help end the spread of AIDS and make treatment available in all countries.

Armed Opposition Groups

Armed opposition groups are combatants in a relatively new type of conflict, fought by one or more armed groups or factions against each other and/or the government. These groups are responsible for a significant number and wide variety of human rights abuses.

Since the end of the Cold War, the map of state relations, conflicts, and arms control has changed considerably. Formerly, wars were mainly fought by two opposing conventional forces. In recent years there has been a proliferation of non-international conflicts, often of an ethnic or religious character. The collapse of state institutions and the increased availability of small arms have also fuelled abuses of human rights of civilians in internal conflicts.

All violations of human rights during conflicts whoever commits them are unacceptable breaches of basic standards of humane behaviour. Armed opposition groups have the international legal obligation to respect fundamental rights, just like government armies do. All parties to the conflict are bound by the provisions of the four Geneva Conventions, which prohibit torture and ill-treatment, hostage taking, and deliberate and arbitrary killing of persons taking no active part in the hostilities. In the dozens of armed conflicts being fought around the world, there is an obvious need for increased protection of individuals. Human rights groups such as Amnesty International have informed the international community about abuses by armed opposition groups in Burundi, Kosovo, Algeria, and India, to name a few.

Attacks on civilians by armed opposition groups are nowhere more prevalent than in Burundi, a small country in eastern Africa. Government forces and armed opposition groups in Burundi are divided largely on ethnic lines, Hutu and Tutsi. Both the government and the armed opposition groups have been responsible for slaughtering tens of thousands of civilians in reprisal attacks. An estimated one hundred thousand Burundian civilians have been killed since 1993 as a direct result of the civil war.

Kosovo, a province in the former Yugoslavia inhabited mainly by ethnic Albanians, endures a brutal conflict that began in early 1998. While the Kosovo Liberation Army (KLA) and other armed opposition groups reportedly fight to end the discrimination against Kosovo Albanians, they also are guilty of human rights abuses, including taking hostages and killing civilians.

Armed conflicts remain an unfortunate reality. The International Committee of the Red Cross (ICRC) and Amnesty International recognize this reality and urge armed groups to ensure forces under their control abide by basic humanitarian principles. They recommend that those in positions of power such as heads of armed groups, political leaders, and the judiciary end human rights abuses and use the Geneva Convention Article 3 as a minimum standard to protect civilians during civil war. The ICRC also works to train combatants and government forces to spare noncombatants by respecting the rules of war.

International efforts are being made to initiate peace processes in countries such as Burundi where armed opposition groups are responsible for severe human rights abuses. Efforts for peace, as well as disarming and demobilizing combatants, and urging those involved in armed struggles to abide by humanitarian law, are important steps toward building cultures where human rights are respected.

Asylum

The principle of asylum, guaranteed by the Universal Declaration of Human Rights, requires that governments provide a place of safety and protection to refugees from other countries. Issues surrounding the rights of individuals to seek asylum and the responsibility of states to provide it are central ones to the human rights movement.

A refugee is a person who, "owing to a well-founded fear of being persecuted for reasons of race, religion, nationality, membership of a particular social group, or political opinion, is outside" the country of citizenship and either can not return home or is fearful of doing so (Convention Relating to the Status of Refugees, 1951). Throughout history, people have faced the necessity of fleeing their homes to seek safety in other countries. The Greeks and the Romans had established areas for refugees, and places of asylum are noted in the Bible. Displacement of large populations has continued to the present. It is important to note that historically, a refugee's legal right extended only to the request for asylum, not a guarantee that it would be granted.

One of the earliest documents in international law dealing with refugees was the Charter of the International Military Tribunal at Nuremberg, which defined forced deportation as a crime against humanity and prosecuted Nazi leaders for pursuing this policy during the Third Reich. Indeed, it was the effort to assist persons fleeing Nazi Germany and the Soviet Union during World War II that evolved into the United Nations High Commission for Refugees (UNHCR). UNHCR operates under the 1951 Convention Relating to the Status of Refugees and its 1967 Protocol.

Currently, several issues are debated regarding refugees and the right to seek asylum. First is the question of *nonrefoulement*, or the right of a refugee not to be returned to a home country engaging in persecution. The policy of *non-refoulement* is controversial because, in practice, it undermines the principle that an asylum seeker is not guaranteed sanctuary. Second is the issue of so-called economic refugees. These are refugees fleeing to another country in order to achieve a higher standard of living; some argue that, strictly speaking, these people should simply be considered migrants.

Finally, in recent years the issue of gender persecution has arisen. Gender has not traditionally been associated with asylum; nonetheless, more and more women are fleeing their home countries to escape female genital mutilation, forced marriages, or the Islamic restrictions on women's freedom of movement known as purdah. In June 1996, after a sixteen-month detention, Fauziya Kassindja was granted asylum in the United States. Kassindja had fled her home in Togo three years earlier to escape genital mutilation and a forced marriage to a polygamist. Although gender had been recognized as a basis for persecution in a few cases prior to this most notably in Canada the Kassindja case was the first U.S. case to recognize gender persecution as a basis for granting asylum.

UNHCR estimates that almost six million refugees have applied for asylum in the last decade. The number of applications peaked in 1993 and has fallen somewhat since then. Nonetheless, there is no indication that the refugee problem and, therefore, questions of asylum, are going to disappear anytime soon.

Bonded Labour

Bonded labour, also known as debt bondage, is a form of debt servitude in which a person works to pay off a debt owed to the employer. The terms of such arrangements are usually so biased in the employer's favour that the bonded labourer, far from settling his or her debt, becomes even more indebted with the passage of time. This allows the debt holder to further consolidate control over the bonded labourer, whose very person becomes the property of the employer as security on the debt. Under these exploitative conditions, the human rights abuses associated with bonded labour have led activists to describe it as a contemporary form of slavery. Though the practice is explicitly prohibited by several major human rights protocols and is illegal according to the laws of many of the nations in which it occurs, enforcement of such laws has proved difficult.

Unlike the historic practice of indentured servitude, to which it is related, bonded labour agreements do not usually specify a period of time during which the debtor will work to settle the outstanding debt. Instead, bonded labourers are paid extremely low wages against which the employer deducts interest on the debt, enormously inflated food and housing costs, and other unilaterally imposed fines or punishments. Persons who enter bonded labour arrangements to pay off a small sum of money then owe progressively greater amounts as their debt bondage perpetuates itself. Security on the debt may pass from one family member to another and from generation to generation, such that very young children may be forced into bonded labour to pay off the debts of their parents.

While adult bonded labor is widespread in countries across Asia, Africa, and Latin America, it is child bonded labor that has attracted the most attention. A specialized agency of the United Nations, the International Labour Organization (ILO), and a host of NGOs are the sponsors of a wide range of initiatives designed to halt the use of child bonded labour, particularly in South Asia where it is most prevalent. In India, where estimates suggest that as many as fifteen million children are held as bonded labourers, children may enter into debt bondage by inheriting a parent's debt, or they may simply be sold to an employer in exchange for a loan to the parent. In a pattern that is repeated around the region, low-caste and indigenous children are particularly at risk because of their parents' poverty, lack of education, and low social status. Some human rights interventions target the use of child bonded labour in particular industries, such as the silk industry in India and the handwoven carpet industry in Pakistan, Nepal, and India. Other interventions target children from vulnerable communities, such as the Dumagat people of the Philippines or the Kamaiya of Nepal.

As part of the ILO's campaign to eliminate the most intolerable forms of child labour, several nations including India, Pakistan, the Philippines, Nepal, and Bangladesh have instituted or strengthened laws prohibiting child bonded labour. However, the sincerity of some governments' commitment is in question, as law enforcement seems more interested in harassing labour and human rights activists than in prosecuting those employers who hold their workers in debt bondage. The ILO plans to introduce a new international convention to further combat the practice of bonded labour. Meanwhile, a growing international movement, sparked in part by the 1995 murder of child labour activist Iqbal Masih, encourages consumers in industrialized nations to shun products made by child bonded labor.

Child Soldiers

The use of children as soldiers has increased dramatically in recent decades. Today it is estimated that more than 300,000 children under the age of eighteen some as young as six years old serve in government armies and armed opposition groups. This practice is in violation of numerous human rights norms, as it puts children at risk for a wide variety of abuses.

In the past both boys and girls have served as support staff and soldiers for Cambodia's Khmer Rouge, for rebel groups in Uganda during the 1970s, and during the civil war in El Salvador in the 1980s. According to the group Human Rights Watch, children participated in thirty-three conflicts in 1996 in twenty six of these, children under the age of fifteen were used as soldiers.

Armies use children for the same reasons they should not: children are more easily manipulated than adults, they often do not understand the implications of war or killing, and they are the most "disposable" to do dangerous jobs such as minesweeping. Children are coerced or conscripted into armies or join "voluntarily" out of fear or poverty. The increased availability of small arms makes it physically more practical for children to fight.

The recruitment of children under the age of fifteen and their participation in hostilities is forbidden by the 1997

Additional Protocols to the Geneva Convention. The UN Convention on the Rights of the Child (CRC) Article 38 stipulates, "Parties shall refrain from recruiting any person who has not attained the age of fifteen into their armed forces." Today most states agree the current minimum age of fifteen for recruitment of soldiers is too low. The International Red Cross, the Red Crescent Movement, and key UN agencies have been working to abolish soldiers under the age of eighteen. In 1994 the UN established a Working Group to draft an optional protocol to the CRC, raising the minimum age from fifteen to eighteen. While the majority of states agree on eighteen as the minimum age, the United States, Korea, Israel, and the United Kingdom are among those who argue that eighteen is too high. No consensus has been reached.

Demobilization and rehabilitation of child soldiers is an onerous task. They usually suffer grave social, emotional, and physical problems and are often the last group of concern for a state that is in the midst of war or has recently ended one. UNICEF and other agencies have begun to tackle the job of demobilization, rehabilitation, and family reunification of former child soldiers in Angola, Rwanda, and Sierra Leone. In southern Sudan, at the request of two rebel movements, Radda Barnen (Swedish Save the Children) has begun a program to assist child soldiers.

The movement to ban the use of child soldiers is growing. National campaigns have formed and in 1998 a new initiative, the Coalition to Stop the Use of Child Soldiers, was launched by Human Rights Watch in conjunction with other nongovernmental agencies to mobilize public opinion and political will to ban the military recruitment and participation in armed conflict of children under the age of eighteen.

Efforts to ban the use of child soldiers reaffirm the principle that children should be allowed to be children and condemns an intolerable practice. All recommendations push for their immediate disarmament and the provision of the assistance for their long path to reintegration into civil society.

Conscientious Objection

Conscientious objection is defined as a refusal to perform military service based on a sincerely held belief that war is morally or ethically wrong. Conscientious objectors (COs) may oppose all forms of war and violence or may oppose certain types of war, like nuclear or chemical warfare. Selective objectors oppose a particular war as "unjust." Whether their opposition to war is based upon religious or secular convictions, COs are denied the right to freedom of conscience in those countries with a compulsory military draft that offer no civilian alternative to military service or that offer punishingly harsh conditions to anyone seeking such an alternative.

The earliest attempts to formalize the rights of COs coincided with the massive military conscriptions of World War I. In the United States, where Christian pacifist churches like the Society of Friends (Quakers) had long preached opposition to war, some attempts were made to legally accommodate conscientious objectors on religious grounds. Though still required to perform military service, religious COs could serve as unarmed noncombatants. But these provisions left no legal options for COs who objected to war on political or secular grounds, or for those whose consciences forbade any participation in military service. Several thousand of these were court-martialed and imprisoned and some remained in prison for years until freed by a presidential pardon in 1933.

Following World War II the leaders of the international peace movement pressed governments to protect their citizens' civil liberties and right to freedom of conscience by making provisions for COs to be legally exempted from military service. This campaign has met with mixed success. The United Nations Human Rights Commission

(UNHRC) recognizes the right to conscientious objection as part of the freedom of thought, conscience, and religion defined in Article 18 of the Universal Declaration of, but more than forty countries with military conscription still do not provide any alternative to armed service. COs who fail to comply with military service orders in these countries face imprisonment, and Amnesty International considers them to be prisoners of conscience.

While growing numbers of nations have abandoned military conscription or have adopted liberal policies regarding COs, many countries still persecute COs. In Greece, where no alternative civilian service exists, more than five hundred men have been imprisoned by military courts for their refusal to join the military. Most of these men are Jehovah's Witnesses, whose religious beliefs expressly forbid any form of military service. In Turkey, where it is a crime to "alienate people from the military," Osman Murat Uelke was prosecuted for "trickery to avoid military service" on the grounds that conscientious objection was not an acceptable concept.

As conscientious objection from military service gains greater recognition as a basic human right, attempts have been made to extend the concept of conscientious objection to other situations where citizens may object to government mandates; for example, health care practitioners may object to certain medical procedures and duties like euthanasia or abortion-on religious or ethical grounds. While it remains to be seen whether these efforts to expand the scope of conscientious objection will garner international recognition, they do offer compelling proof that the peace movement has succeeded in making conscientious objection a potent symbol of the right to freedom of conscience.

Cultural Rights

Cultural rights are concerned with creating and ensuring

the conditions that allow people to participate in and contribute to the cultural life of their communities. Described as the requirements for human dignity and development, cultural rights were originally understood as the rights of individuals to share in education, information, science, and art. But cultural rights have been more recently understood as the rights of peoples usually ethnic, linguistic, or religious minorities to freely practice their own culture as a community. Current debates about cultural rights are driven by the unresolved tension between those who argue that human rights can only exist at the level of the individual (the conventional Western understanding of rights) and those who say that groups of people can collectively be the object of human rights protections.

Cultural rights were established in 1948 by the Universal Declaration of Human Rights. Specific cultural rights are represented in two articles of the declaration: Article 26, on the right to education, and Article 27, on copyright protection and the right to participate in cultural life. These rights were elaborated upon and introduced into the formal body of international law by the International Covenant on Economic, Social and Cultural Rights (ICESCR) created in 1966 by the United Nations General Assembly.

The effort to translate the ideals promoted by the ICESCR from prescriptions into action has met with some difficulties. Many international legal experts believe that cultural rights like the right to education are of minor importance compared to the urgency of civil and political rights like freedom from torture. Others have declared that economic, social, and cultural rights are not human rights at all, but unenforceable demands that governments pursue an idealistic and by no means unanimously shared model of social justice.

In the past decade a vocal group of Asian nations including Singapore, Malaysia, and Indonesia has argued that the Western emphasis on civil and political rights reflects a cultural bias not shared by the developing nations of Asia, Africa, and Latin America. As developing nations demand a greater voice in determining the international standards of conduct, they draw renewed attention to the concepts of economic, social, and cultural rights, which they claim hold greater urgency for the citizens of impoverished countries.

This attention has coincided with a new conceptualization of cultural rights to include the rights of minority groups. The focus on the rights of a minority community, rather than on the rights of individual persons belonging to a minority, has come under considerable criticism. Critics argue that laws promoting the interests of a cultural minority grant unfair special privileges, sparking sometimes virulent resentment among members of the majority culture. The increasing reluctance of the English-speaking provinces of western Canada to grant special status to French speaking Quebec and Quebec's threat to secede if Canada does not provide adequate protection to Francophone culture illustrate both the hazards and the importance of cultural rights in a multicultural society. A related issue is whether the granting of cultural rights to a community may disable protections for individual rights, particularly in cases where the community observes cultural customs that may violate the human rights of some of its members, as in exclusionary caste systems or female genital mutilation. Though these dilemmas hamper efforts to define or enforce a common standard for cultural rights, it is clear that, as ethnic violence increases around the world, finding solutions to the issues raised by cultural rights will be of primary importance.

Death Penalty

The death penalty is generally conceived of as the supreme legal sanction, inflicted only against perpetrators of the most serious crimes. The human rights community has traditionally held a stance against the death penalty for a wide variety of reasons: critics argue that the death penalty is inhuman and degrading; that it is inappropriately applied and often politically motivated; and that rather than reducing crime, the viciousness of the punishment only serves as an inspiration to further violence.

Historically the death penalty has existed all around the world. Only since the beginning of the twentieth century has the death penalty been rejected by a growing number of people and states.

International law discourages but does not prohibit it. Article 6 (paragraphs 2 and 5) of the International Covenant on Civil and Political Rights states that "sentence of death may be imposed only for the most serious crimes in accordance with the law in force at the time of the commission of the crime. Sentence of death shall not be imposed for crimes committed by persons below eighteen years of age and shall not be carried out on pregnant women." Regarding the non-reintroduction of the death penalty, the American Convention on Human Rights (Article 4.3) is the most explicit instrument, since it provides that "[t]he death penalty shall not be re-established in states that have abolished it."

Although the death penalty is not entirely prohibited, several legal instruments have been brought into existence that seem to pave the way for total abolition. The Second Optional Protocol to the International Covenant on Civil and Political Rights aims at the abolition of the death penalty, by virtue of which thirty-three states have decided to abolish this punishment within their jurisdiction. It is in the European system that the trend has gone the furthest. The Convention for the Protection of Human Rights and Fundamental Freedoms now has a Protocol No. 6 Concerning the Abolition of the Death Penalty. This was adopted in 1982 by the Council of Europe's Committee of Ministers.

According to data presented at the 1998 session of the Sub-Commission on Prevention of Discrimination and Protection of Minorities, fifty-four states have abolished the death penalty and fifteen others have done the same except in times of war. Twenty-seven additional states no longer apply the sentence, although it has not been made illegal. Finally, ninety-seven states maintain the death penalty in their legal systems. According to 1996 Amnesty International figures, China, the Ukraine, the Russian Federation, and Iran had the highest number of executions, accounting for 92 percent of the year's total. Although the execution of people under age eighteen is prohibited by international law, five nations have been accused by Amnesty International of continuing the practice–Iran, Pakistan, Saudi Arabia, the United States, and Yemen.

A death penalty carried out unlawfully comes under the competence of the Special Rapporteur on Summary and Arbitrary Executions elected by the UN Commission on Human Rights. The UN Secretary General, when apprised of impending executions that may not conform to the above-mentioned safeguards, can use his best endeavours, as he did in vain in 1986 with an appeal for the life of James Terry Roche. Roche was later executed in the United States for murder committed when he was seventeen.

Among NGOs, Amnesty International has taken a leading role in pursuing abolition of the death penalty worldwide. The group argues that the death penalty is "an act of violence and violence tends to provoke violence. The imposition and infliction of the death penalty is brutalizing to all who are involved in the process." In 1998 Amnesty International protested the execution of Karla Faye Tucker in Texas, issuing a scathing critique of the Texas justice system, accusing it of "a litany of grossly inadequate procedures which fail to meet minimum international standards for the protection of human rights."

Apart from humanitarian and philosophical concerns, the most striking argument against the death penalty seems to be the fact that, as euphemistically stated by successive United Nations studies, "the deterrent effect of the death penalty is, to say the least, not demonstrated." However, the debate is still lively, as supporters of the death penalty remain firmly convinced that the punishment is a necessary and effective method of controlling crime.

With respect to the death penalty, the challenges ahead are still numerous, but the most fundamental goes beyond the legal sphere nations must grapple with whether or not "an-eye-for-an-eye" is the doctrine best suited to bring about justice.

Detention

Detention occurs when a person is deprived of his or her personal liberty and confined to a space, usually a jail cell, prison, hospital, or home. Detention differs from imprisonment in that detainees, unlike prisoners, have not been convicted of a criminal offense. The tremendous vulnerability of detainees to human rights abuses, and the threat that detentions pose to the basic right to liberty, have led to strict international laws governing the use of detention. Nevertheless many governments routinely ignore the international restrictions on the use of detention, and reports issued by many human rights organizations suggest that human rights abuses related to detention are prevalent around the world.

Detailed regulations on detention were established by the International Covenant on Civil and Political Rights and the regional European Convention on Human Rights, the American Convention on Human Rights (1969), and the African Charter on Human and People's Rights (1981). These regulations prohibit arbitrary detention, which is defined as any deprivation of personal liberty not justified by and conducted according to previously existing laws. In nations that do not have or do not enforce adequate legal controls over their police or military, arbitrary detention becomes a potent weapon to punish, coerce, or intimidate citizens.

Detention may be used to hold persons who have been accused of committing a crime but have not yet been tried in a court of law for the offense. The ICCPR sets certain conditions for the appropriate use of pretrial detention: a detained person must be immediately informed of the charges against him or her, must be promptly brought before a judicial power, and should be brought to trial within a reasonable amount of time. However, lack of resources, inefficient or overburdened judicial systems, and in some cases, deliberate government foot-dragging make excessive lengths of pretrial detention a human rights issue in many countries where detainees may wait more than two years before standing trial.

Administrative detention, in which a country's legal system specifically allows persons to be detained without charge or trial, is a controversial practice in several countries. For example, according to Israeli law, the government may hold persons indefinitely if evidence suggests that they pose a danger to state security. Several hundred Palestinians from Israel and the Occupied Territories and in recent years a handful of Jews as well have been held incommunicado in administrative detention for months or even years without charge or trial. In many cases no credible evidence links the detainees to any terrorist activity, leading Amnesty International and other monitoring groups to conclude that Israel, which ratified the ICCPR in 1991, detains prisoners of conscience for the peaceful expression of their beliefs.

The United States has also been the target of criticism for its use of administrative detention to confine refugees seeking asylum. The Immigration and Naturalization Service (INS) may detain illegal immigrants and candidates for asylum indefinitely. Contrary to the explicit conditions established by the ICCPR, which the United States ratified in 1992, INS detainees not convicted of any crime may be imprisoned in local jails alongside convicted criminals. The publicity surrounding abuses of detention even in Western democracies suggests that the movement to enforce international standards of conduct regarding detention, most recently reiterated in a 1988 United Nations statement on the protections due detained or imprisoned persons, will continue to gain momentum in the future.

Development

Development has traditionally been defined as a process promoting economic growth. But in recent years the international community has pioneered a new understanding in which the aim of development is not merely to produce better results in the leading economic indicators but to improve the quality of life in every sphere of meaningful activity: economic, social, cultural, and political. Using these expanded criteria for successful development, the United Nations issued a landmark Declaration on the Right to Development in 1986, establishing development as a basic human right and demanding that other human rights concerns be integrated with development programs.

Human rights played a tenuous role in the early international development programs created after World War II. Under the Marshall Plan (1948-51), the United States provided billions of dollars in development aid to reconstruct the economies of postwar Europe and encourage European nations to resist communism. In the 1950s and 1960s U.S. aid to the impoverished nations of postcolonial Asia, Africa, and Latin America frequently bypassed struggling local populations, instead enriching corrupt authoritarian but anticommunist regimes. Meanwhile, multilateral development agencies like the World Bank and the United Nations Development Program encouraged large industrial projects that provided few benefits to the poor but destabilized indigenous cultures, caused environmental degradation, or siphoned local wealth to Western business interests.

The 1970s marked the beginning of a major change in attitudes toward development. Most sweeping was the rise of the concept of "sustainable development." Born out of a growing concern for the harmful consequences of industrial development to local ecosystems, sustainable development proposed a more holistic model that balanced the potential economic benefits of a project against its ecological costs. Expanding views also encouraged an increasing attention to the social and cultural changes wrought by development. Where previous theories treated development as a phenomenon in isolation, whose effects could be calculated solely in economic terms, advocates of the holistic approach to development viewed economic activity as only one element of a complex, interconnected system.

Not surprisingly, one effect of these development theories was to increase awareness of the human rights implications of development work. Organizations like the World Bank began to place more emphasis on aiding vulnerable populations, while the United States under President Jimmy Carter (1977-1981) tried to link development aid to the recipient nation's human rights record, threatening to end development aid to repressive regimes like Argentina's military junta.

The Declaration on the Right to Development issued by the UN General Assembly signalled another significant shift in approaches to development. The declaration defined development as a human centered process that should ideally enlarge the choices of individuals and communities while respecting the principles of self-determination, equity, and nondiscrimination. In trying to translate these principles into concrete action, the international community faces the difficult task of bridging the chasm between "developing" and "developed" nations, a task made more complicated by increasing globalization and the dominant economic power of multinational corporations. More than ever, providing the basic human rights called for in the Universal Declaration of Human Rights such as access to employment and an adequate standard of living will require international cooperation and a commitment to pursue sustainable and fair development policies.

Disappearances

The term "disappearance" describes the secret arrest, detention, or abduction of a person by government officials or groups acting with the approval or knowledge of the government. The practice of disappearance is a direct violation of several key principles of human rights, outlined in the Universal Declaration and other instruments.

The term *desaparecido* (disappeared) was first coined in the 1960s in Guatemala to label the state-sponsored kidnapping, torture, and murder of antigovernment forces. In the 1960s, '70s, and '80s, disappearances were also reported in Argentina, Chile, El Salvador, and Uruguay. In these and other countries, relatives of the disappeared organized in an attempt to locate the missing and to raise awareness of the issue. The first and most famous of these organizations was the Mothers of the Plaza in Argentina. In the late 1970s these mothers and their allies began demonstrating weekly in the *Plaza de Mayo*. They were instrumental in raising international awareness of the practice of disappearance.

In 1980 the United Nations established the Working Group on Enforced or Involuntary Disappearances. In the past two decades the Working Group has investigated more than fifty thousand individual disappearances. In 1992 the United Nations General Assembly adopted the Declaration on the Protection of All Persons from Enforced Disappearance, which stated that enforced disappearance is an offense to human dignity and that no state should practice nor allow enforced disappearances. The Working Group is responsible for monitoring compliance with the declaration; in its 1997 report, the group noted that state conformity with the declaration has been slow.

Although the term *desaparecido* was coined in response to the large number of disappearances in Latin America, disappearances have been reported all around the world; in fact, the Working Group is investigating disappearances in seventy countries. For example, they are currently researching more than 450 disappearances in the Philippines since 1970. Afghanistan, Cambodia, Equatorial Guinea, Ethiopia, Morocco, Sri Lanka, Turkey, and Uganda have all been accused of the systematic use of disappearance. In addition, while some professions are targeted more than others-politicians, journalists, and human rights advocates, for example people from all walks of life have been disappeared.

Although disappearance is widely considered a violation of human rights law, few perpetrators are punished for the crime. First, few countries have implemented laws specifically addressing disappearance, as called for in the declaration. Second, disappearances frequently occur in the context of civil war or unrest. When conflicts cease, perpetrators may go unpunished because general amnesty is granted in conjunction with peace accords. Finally, even when no such amnesty is granted, new governments, hoping to put the civil unrest behind them, frequently grant pardons to those convicted of causing disappearances. The issue of impunity exempting those who cause disappearances from punishment for their crimes is becoming especially important as more and more proof of disappearance becomes available.

The Working Group, along with a variety of NGOs, is calling for the implementation of national laws against disappearance, as mandated by the Declaration, as well as international legal norms naming forced disappearance as a violation of international human rights law.

Extradition

Extradition is the official surrender of fugitive offenders from one state to the jurisdiction of another, for the purpose of criminal prosecution or the execution of a sentence. This procedure is part of a broader framework of international cooperation in criminal matters. It is related to human rights for two reasons: first, it helps to achieve international cooperation in the punishment of perpetrators of human rights violations; second, an extradition carried out without due process violates international human rights norms.

Historically, international cooperation on the subject of fugitives dates back to the beginning of formal diplomacy. In 1833 Belgium was the first nation to pass extradition legislation, which outlined the circumstances and methods through which extradition might occur. At first extradition involved primarily political refugees. However, this trend evolved such that extradition procedures now cover "common" criminals, rather than refugees.

The sources of contemporary extradition law may be found in multilateral or bilateral treaties (such as the European Convention on Extradition of 1957), as well as in national extradition policies. There is no worldwide extradition convention. The duty to extradite exists only if a treaty has established the obligation thereof. In the absence of a treaty, the domestic law of the state in question may solely determine whether extradition is permitted and under what conditions.

There are, however, certain substantive principles that can be found in most extradition instruments. For example, the double-criminality rule requires that a person may be extradited only if the act that she or he allegedly committed is a crime under both of the involved states' laws. Another important rule is the specialty rule, which forbids the state seeking extradition (called the requesting state) to punish the person to be extradited for any offense committed prior to the extradition, other than the offense for which he was extradited.

Concurrently, most extradition treaties provide for a number of exceptions to the obligation to extradite. Some states (e.g., Germany, the Netherlands, and France) refuse to extradite their own nationals. It was for this reason that Libya refused to extradite two of its nationals allegedly responsible for the explosion of an airplane over Lockerbie, Scotland. Extradition may also be denied if the offense for which it is requested is punishable by death in the legislation of the requesting state. Humanitarian considerations (due to the age or health of the person to be extradited, for example) may also lead a state to refuse extradition. Likewise, states may refuse to extradite someone for political offenses although the definition of political offenses raises many problems, as it varies from state to state. Finally, the discrimination clause, contained for the first time in the European Convention on Extradition of 1957, forbids extradition if the request is motivated by the individual's race, religion, or political opinion.

It is also worth mentioning that some treaties (such as the Geneva Conventions of 1949 and its First 1977 Additional Protocol) provide for aut dedere aut judicare, which means "to prosecute or to extradite." This obligation is the procedural consequence of the principle of universal jurisdiction, which allows a state to try a person regardless of his or her nationality or where the offense was committed. Universal jurisdiction also exists under customary international law in relation to certain international crimes, such as genocide or crimes against humanity.

In 1998 controversy raged over the fate of former Chilean dictator General Augusto Pinochet, who was arrested in London while recuperating from surgery. Spain issued an international warrant for Pinochet's arrest and requested that he be extradited to Madrid to stand trial for genocide, torture, and terrorism, specifically crimes committed against Spanish nationals under his regime. As of this writing, the procedure is still pending. But regardless of the outcome, the arrest itself was hailed as the dawn of a new era in international cooperation in the prosecution of human rights violators.

With the current development of international criminal law through the creation of ad hoc and permanent international criminal courts and an increased willingness on the part of the international community to prosecute human rights offenses, it is evident that the problem of extradition will continue to be of importance.

Extrajudicial Executions

The carrying out of an execution without prior fair trial and without respect for fundamental judicial guarantees is shocking for those concerned with human rights. The concept of extrajudicial executions (also called summary or arbitrary executions) has been addressed by a variety of international legal instruments. According to author Nigel S. Rodley, "Most simply, summary or arbitrary executions are officially sanctioned murder."

Extrajudicial executions first began to be perceived as problematic with the development and acceptance of the rule of law as the basis for liberal democracy, subsequent to the French and American Revolutions. Summary executions obviously infringe on the right to life, but also on the presumption of innocence and the right to a fair trial. The factors conducive to extrajudicial executions are as varied as the states that engage in the practice some causes include the absence of a democratic political process, the existence of a state of emergency, the lack of judicial independence, or the existence of secret police or paramilitary groups. Extrajudicial executions are not isolated acts; the practice is, unfortunately, very widespread.

Several human rights instruments prohibit extrajudicial executions. Article 6.1 of the International Covenant on Civil and Political Rights provides that "no one shall be arbitrarily deprived of his life." The Principles on the Effective Prevention and Investigation of Extra-Legal, Arbitrary, and Summary Executions, adopted by the Economic and Social Council (ECOSOC) in 1989, constitute standards for implementing this article of the covenant. Governments are to guarantee effective protection to groups or individuals in danger of such execution. Moreover, the principles require a thorough, prompt, and impartial investigation of all suspected cases of summary or arbitrary executions. In times of war, the Geneva Conventions of 1949 and its protocols also provide for judicial guarantees that can reduce the occurrence of extrajudicial executions.

In 1982 the UN Commission on Human Rights designated the first Special Rapporteur on Summary or

Arbitrary Executions. He is charged to examine the questions related to summary or arbitrary executions and to report annually to the commission. His reports usually denounce violations and the responsible governments with precision.

The challenge of the future fight against extrajudicial executions is not the establishment of new legal standards, because many solid ones exist. Rather the international community must achieve better implementation and enforcement of existing rules.

Female Genital Mutilation

Female genital mutilation (FGM) is the name given to the surgical operation in which part, or all, of the external female genitalia is removed; it is also known as female circumcision. Those who denounce FGM say that it is a violent human rights abuse against women, while proponents say that it is an important cultural tradition that must be preserved.

It is estimated that 80 to 135 million females around the world have undergone FGM, usually between the ages of four and twelve, and at present there are some two million girls at risk each year. The practice occurs in Africa, the Middle East, parts of Asia, and in immigrant communities in Europe and North America. In its mildest form, the clitoris is partially or totally removed. In the most extreme form, called infibulation, the clitoris, labia minora, labia majora, and the urethral and vaginal openings are cut away. The vagina is then stitched or held together, leaving a small opening for menstruation and urination. Cutting and restitching may be necessary for childbirth and sexual intercourse. The operation is commonly performed by untrained practitioners, with no form of anesthetic, and cutting instruments include broken glass, tin lids, scissors, or unsterilized razors. In addition to causing intense pain, the procedure carries with it a number of health risks such as pelvic infections, hemorrhaging, obstructed labour and childbirth, and the spread of HIV.

Typical arguments supporting FGM are that it will reduce promiscuity, increase cleanliness, and enhance femininity. In cultures where FGM is common, marriage prospects are higher for a woman who has undergone the procedure. In some communities it is believed that the clitoris will eventually hang down between a woman's legs unless it is removed. All of the reasons are cultural and traditional and are not rooted in any religious texts.

Frequently there is opposition to outside intervention in communities where FGM is practiced. Western interference can be seen as cultural imperialism, and some ask the rhetorical question, "What right do others have to criticize our way of life?" Some supporters of FGM point to Western practices that they find immoral, such as giving up children for adoption, sending parents to elderly homes, or conducting abortions. Another barrier to foreign involvement is that family members, friends, and relatives apply pressure on young women to undergo FGM, and view the issue as an entirely private family matter.

Nevertheless, the issue of FGM has garnered increasing global attention over the past several years. Nongovernmental organizations like Amnesty International are conducting research and campaign work on FGM. The U.S. government has taken steps to criminalize FGM in America and now considers asylum applications in light of FGM practices in the country of origin. In April 1997 the heads of three UN agencies the World Health Organization, the United Nations Population Fund, and the United Nations Children's Fund issued a joint plea for the eradication of FGM, saying it would be a major step forward in the promotion of human rights worldwide.

Gender-Related Persecution

Gender-related persecution is the oppression of women because of their gender. It includes a variety of gender-specific human rights infringements, including forced pregnancy, forced abortion, and female genital mutilation, as well as offenses that are chiefly directed at women, such as rape and domestic abuse.

The earliest human rights protections afforded to women came in the context of their roles as mothers or future mothers; women were not supposed to do heavy labour, work in mines, or work at night. After years of agitation, women's suffrage came into effect in most European countries and North America during the early twentieth century (1920 in the United States). In 1945 the Charter of the United Nations went into effect, and for the first time the human rights of women were afforded equal status with the human rights of men.

Although women's human rights were, therefore, technically part of international law, it was the Convention on the Elimination of All Forms of Discrimination Against Women (CEDAW) in 1979 that standardized women's human rights. CEDAW addresses the human rights of women in several different contexts, covering women's private and public lives; it has been ratified by more than 160 countries, but not the United States. The greatest drawback to CEDAW is the large number of reservations submitted by CEDAW signatories. These reservations allow members to exempt themselves from implementing some of the most fundamental aspects of CEDAW, including the elimination of discrimination in political life, equal citizenship rights, full legal capacity, and the elimination of discrimination in marriage and family.

Although women have made significant gains, they still make up a disproportionate number of the world's poor, illiterate, victimized, and marginalized. Globally, their political participation remains small. And while women in some parts of the world enjoy increasing freedom every day, fundamentalist regimes elsewhere persecute women, imposing gender based restrictions on every aspect of their daily lives. In Afghanistan, which as of this writing is controlled by Islamic extremists called the Taliban, women are not allowed to go to work or attend school; they are only allowed to leave their houses when covered from head to toe and accompanied by a man, and they are forbidden from wearing white socks or shoes that make noise. Women who violate the edicts risk harassment, arrest, and severe beatings.

At the 1995 United Nations Women's Conference in Beijing, China, delegates identified poverty as the single greatest obstacle to ending gender-based persecution. Among the other issues addressed by the conference were the education of women and girls, violence against women, political rights, economic rights, women in war zones, medical and health issues, the environment, and the rights of the girl child. In recent years women have organized internationally around several other gender persecution issues. Among these are the fight to recognize gender persecution as a basis for granting asylum; the struggle to prosecute wartime rape as a crime against humanity; the effort to understand domestic violence as a form of torture; and the attempt to reconcile cultural and religious traditions with women's human rights.

While conventions and declarations provide moral and political force to women's human rights, and while governments must continue to demand an end to gender persecution, among the most significant advances made in recent years is increased international organizing and coalition-building by and among women. Today it is women themselves who direct the elimination of gender persecution by demanding, defining, and defending their human rights.

Genocide

Genocide is the deliberate destruction of a national, ethnic, racial, or religious group. The word is from the Greek *genos*, which means race or tribe, and the Latin *cide*, which means killing, and was coined by jurist Raphael Lemkin in response to the Holocaust.

While there have been numerous incidents of genocide throughout human history, the international community first acknowledged a legal concept for this phenomenon in 1948, when the United Nations General Assembly approved the Convention on the Prevention and Punishment of the Crime of Genocide. This convention, also known as the Genocide Convention, states that the following acts, when "committed with intent to destroy, in whole or in part, a national, ethnic, racial or religious group," constitute genocide: killing members of the group; causing serious bodily or mental harm to members of the group; deliberately inflicting conditions of life calculated to bring about the physical destruction of the group; preventing births within the group; and forcibly transferring children of the group to another group.

Closer analysis of the Genocide Convention reveals key elements of its role in international law. Genocide is distinct from other grave international crimes such as "crimes against humanity" or "war crimes" because it is criminal both in peace and war. The convention affirms that genocide is not an internal matter, even if committed by a government on its own territory, but an international one.

Rows of human skulls, on display at the Tuol Sleng Museum of Genocidal Crimes, a former Khmer Rouge torture prison in Phnom Penh, Cambodia (CORBIS/Chris Rainier).

And the convention clarifies that the destruction of a particular group is not genocide *per se:* the term is only applicable if the "intent to destroy" the group is demonstrated. In other words, the individuals must be targeted because they were members of that particular group if the act is to be considered genocidal.

One modern example of genocide occurred in 1994 in Rwanda, where 500,000 to one million members of the Tutsi minority (and some moderate Hutus) were deliberately exterminated. Human rights abuses were committed on a massive scale, including the rape and sexual mutilation of women, which left them physically unable to reproduce. The International Criminal Tribunal for Rwanda (ICTR) was established to try those involved in the killings, and in 1998 (fifty years after the Genocide Convention was approved) it handed down the first conviction for genocide by an international court. It was also the first time that sexual violence was found to be an act of genocide, because it was "committed with the intent to destroy" a particular group.

The United Nations and nongovernmental organizations around the world are currently working on the establishment of a permanent International Criminal Court (ICC). At present the principal judicial organ of the United Nations is the International Court of Justice, whose jurisdiction is restricted to states only. The ICC would be the first permanent global court that could try any individuals, without geographical or chronological limits, for war crimes, crimes against humanity, and genocide, and possibly deter future genocidal massacres.

Girl Children

A preference for boy children is deeply entrenched, to some degree, in nearly every country in the world. Therefore, while the human rights of women and the human rights of children have been addressed by the international community, the human rights of the girl child is a relatively new concern. Because they are usually at home, hidden from public view, it has been easy to overlook the human rights of girls.

In many parts of the world, the sex ratio is artificially skewed in favor of boy children. Recently, the number of males has increased and the number of females has decreased in China, India, Pakistan, and South Korea. In some cases, girl children are so devalued that they are abandoned or killed at birth. Female infanticide the intentional killing of girl babies has been widely documented in China and India, and is believed to be common in other Asian countries. Current technology allows women to know the gender of their fetuses before birth, and in many parts of the world, female fetuses are several thousand times more likely to be aborted than males.

If they are allowed to live, girl children often receive little food and no health care or education all of which are violations of the gifts' human rights. Because girls are less often educated than boys, two-thirds of the world's illiterate adults are women. In many countries girls are more likely to become ill, but less likely to be taken to a doctor than their male counterparts. Discrimination against girl children manifests itself in a variety of more subtle ways as well. In some cultures, for example, although girl children may not be denied an education, they often receive less attention in school and are steered into stereotypical areas of study.

Cultural practices are currently an important human rights issue for girl children. In many parts of the world, girl children are raider the complete and total control of their fathers. A father may treat his daughter however he sees fit even kill her and no one, not even the government, will interfere. In many Asian and African countries, fathers arrange their daughters' marriages: if it benefits the family, girls may be married as young as nine years old. Female genital mutilation, early marriage, and systematic seclusion (called purdah) are all practices that are damaging to girl children but are also cultural traditions.

Discrimination against girl children is so deeply ingrained on an international level UN Convention on the Rights of the Child (CRC). The convention was nearly opened for signature in 1990 containing only male pronouns: "she" and "her" had to be added at the last minute. Given this, it is perhaps not surprising that the convention often does not speak to the special needs of girl children. For example, it does not address female genital mutilation, son preference, or early marriage practices that impact girls more than boys.

Currently, a variety of movements throughout the world are promoting a convention aimed specifically at the rights of girl children. This convention would blend protections from the women's and children's conventions, as well as addressing issues that are currently overlooked by both treaties.

Homelessness

Adequate housing is widely agreed upon to be a basic human right, but it is believed that more than 100 million people in the world today are homeless. Some homeless are refugees or internally displaced persons (IDPs), some have been forcibly evicted from their homes, and some are unable to find and keep shelter for economic or other reasons. If the number of people living in inadequate and unsafe housing is included, the total rises to almost 1.2 billion. This issue, therefore, affects one-quarter of the world's population.

The right to housing has been a part of human rights law since the founding of the United Nations in 1945. Article 25 of the Universal Declaration of Human Rights, adopted by the General Assembly in 1948, states that everyone has the right to a standard of living adequate for health and well-being, and that this standard includes housing. The issue is discussed further in the International Covenant on Economic, Social and Cultural Rights. Promotion of housing along with other economic and social rights has lagged behind the promotion of civil and political rights.

In the United Nations, the Committee on Economic, Social, and Cultural Rights has determined that the right to housing is legally guaranteed under the covenant; a major function of the committee is to oversee governmental compliance. In addition, from 1992 to 1995, a Special Rapporteur on Housing operated under the mandate of the committee. Two of the specific issues the committee and the rapporteur have addressed in recent years are refugees and displaced persons, and forced evictions.

There are currently approximately fifteen million refugees worldwide, usually forced to leave their countries of citizenship because their human rights are in jeopardy. Civil and ethnic wars have also resulted in twenty-five to thirty million more IDPs-people who are displaced within their own countries. Natural disasters also create refugees and displaced persons. According to international human rights standards, the countries to which refugees flee are responsible for providing decent housing to all people within their borders. Nearly two thirds of these refugees are in Asia and Africa, creating huge strains on the resources in those areas.

In 1997 the United Nations expanded protection from forcible eviction. Of special concern are residents who are evicted in connection with international events, such as the Olympic Games. It was alleged in 1996 that thousands were evicted in Atlanta to make way for Olympic structures. In Korea, more than 700,000 people were evicted in Seoul as the country prepared for the 1988 Olympics. In addition, Brazil, Israel, Nigeria, and the Philippines have been accused in recent years of participating in wide-scale forced evictions. Where previously, only governments were restricted from forcibly evicting people from their homes, now governments are held responsible for monitoring the private sector as well.

In June 1996 a global plan of action, produced by the World Conference on Human Settlements II, expanded governments' responsibilities to foster their citizens' right to housing. As with many other human rights issues, a great deal of the work is done by NGOs in individual countries; nonetheless, strong international backing is vitally important to these organizations. There is still some resistance by Western nations to the notion of economic rights, such as housing. However, as non-Western states gain more influence over human rights standards, housing and other economic, social, and cultural rights will grow in prominence.

Human Rights Activists

Members of human rights groups, lawyers, journalists,

relatives who protect victims, and others who act to uphold human rights often become victims themselves. Human rights activists, also known as human rights defenders, have been silenced by threats, imprisonment, disappearance, torture, and death. Recognition of the precarious nature of the work of human rights activists is imperative if they are to be protected in their struggles.

All human beings, including those who defend rights, are guaranteed basic rights under the Universal Declaration of Human Rights of 1948 and international treaties such as the International Covenant on Civil and Political Rights. Rights afforded to all citizens, such as the freedom of thought, conscience, and religion, the right to meet and assemble, and the right to form and join trade unions, are especially relevant to human rights activists.

However, governments often fail to protect activists, despite the national and international laws intended to safeguard them. Cases of violations are shockingly widespread. In March 1997 both the translator and publisher of the 1995 Human Rights Watch report on human rights violations in Turkey were accused of "defaming and belittling the state military and security forces" by the Turkish government. Ertu Rul Kurkau and Ay Enur Zarakolu were found guilty of defamation and were sentenced to ten months in prison and a fine. The punishment meted out to human rights defenders can be extreme. In Honduras, Ernesto Sandoval Bustillo, president of the Human Rights Committee (CODEH) for the region of Santa Rosa de Copan, was executed without trial in February 1998.

For over a decade, a working group of the UN Commission on Human Rights has been negotiating a draft declaration on the rights of human rights defenders which would reaffirm and strengthen the rights of those who work towards the elimination of human rights violations. Obstructions by governments during these negotiations are proof of the challenges in adopting such a declaration. In 1997 Cuba and China proposed wording that restricted defenders to defending only their own rights. Another challenge was a refusal by some governments to recognize the rights of groups to financial resources in the defense of human rights.

On March 4, 1998, the draft declaration was finally adopted by consensus. The final text must still be approved. Fifty years after the adoption of the Universal Declaration of Human Rights, human rights are violated around the world every day. Continued efforts to fortify the legitimacy and protection of those who struggle to realize these fundamental rights are necessary so human rights violators will continue to be challenged.

Independent Judiciary

A judiciary is composed of all the judges who sit on the courts of a given country. Maintaining the independence of the judiciary is an important human rights issue because in order for justice to be served, judges must base all decisions purely on the law, allowing no other external influences from governments, businesses, organizations, or individuals. Judges should not stand to gain or lose anything from their decisions, nor fear retaliation for unpopular legal opinions.

Judicial independence in many countries around the world stems largely from the development of the judiciary in England. Until the late 1600s the king or queen could remove judges from office with no justification required. Growing concern over fairness in taxes, punishments, and individual rights led to the formulation of laws that protected the independence of judges. By 1700, judges could not be dismissed as long as they conducted their duties in accordance with the law.

Judicial independence is a cornerstone for the protection of human rights in any society, as true justice cannot be administered without it. Today there exists an international standard for state judiciaries, set out in the Basic Principles on the Independence of the Judiciary, which was adopted by the UN General Assembly in 1985. These principles explicitly state that judges must be selected impartially and must decide cases based on law and the facts of the case, without improper inducements, pressures, or interference.

Countries that do not measure up to the standards delineated in the basic principles fall under close scrutiny by the international community. In 1994 the UN Commission on Human Rights noted the "link between the weakening of safeguards for the judiciary, and the gravity and frequency of violations of human rights" and established a Special rapporteur, a type of investigator, on the Independence of Judges and Lawyers. The rapporteur meets with governments, nongovernmental organizations, and intergovernmental organizations to report on the state of judicial independence.

In one typical example, the government of Bahrain's judiciary allowed the imprisonment of a prominent human rights lawyer, Ahmad Al-Shamlan, in 1996 without charge or trial. It was suspected that he was incarcerated because of his advocacy for human rights victims. The rapporteur intervened, using the documentation of the case to show that there was no legal basis for his imprisonment and that the government had openly applied pressure to the judiciary. Shortly thereafter Al-Shamlan was released with no charges brought against him. The rapporteur documented and publicized the flaws in the Bahraini legal system, which allows judges to be influenced by factors outside the law. In situations such as these, the UN continues its monitoring of the situation, with the ultimate aim of meeting all the standards set by international norms.

In the 1990s there has been increasing worldwide agreement on implementing international standards, as evidenced by regional judicial conferences in Asia, Latin America, Africa, and Europe. While each country is different, it appears that judges around the globe vigorously support the protection of free and fair courts for all.

Indigenous Peoples

The particular human rights concerns of indigenous peoples have only been recognized in recent years. Representatives of these groups have identified many common goals, such as the right to religions, languages, educational institutions, possession or use of indigenous lands and natural resources, and self-determination.

At present there are approximately four thousand indigenous groups, with a population of 200 to 350 million people, living in more than seventy countries of the world. The many indigenous peoples that populate the globe include the Mayans of Guatemala, the Saami of northern Europe, the Hmong of Laos, the Kuna of Panama, the Aborigines and Torres Strait Islanders of Australia, and the Inuit and Aleutians of the circumpolar region.

Indigenous communities are defined as those with a historical continuity tied to precolonization land and the societies that developed on their territories. They have retained social, cultural, economic, and political characteristics that are distinct from those of the other segments of the national population. Often their native language is different from that of the rest of society. Self-identification is seen as a crucial factor for recognizing an indigenous group. Although they may or may not comprise a numerical minority, they typically form a nondominant sector of society it is often this minority status that makes it easy, even tempting, for states to violate their human rights.

Indigenous peoples have some protection under international law. The most prominent treaty is the Convention Concerning Indigenous and Tribal Peoples in Independent Countries, known as the International Labour Organization (ILO) Convention 169, which was adopted in 1989. The World Bank has also recognized that indigenous peoples have a right to special protection and has developed an operational directive that defines policies and procedures that will uphold the rights of indigenous peoples. And in Latin America, the Inter-American Commission on Human Rights proposed an American Declaration on the Rights of Indigenous Peoples in 1997.

Indigenous rights only became internationally recognized within the last three decades and are increasingly garnering attention from the international community. In the 1920s a group of American Indians approached the League of Nations in Geneva to raise the issue of indigenous rights, but this initiative produced little or no results. In 1948 the Bolivian government attempted to create a body in the UN to study the problems of indigenous populations, but again the effort did not come to fruition. In 1970 human rights experts in the UN agreed that the rights of indigenous peoples had been ignored for too long and appointed a Special Rapporteur to study the problems of indigenous peoples.

In 1982 the UN established a Working Group on Indigenous Populations (WGIP) which has conducted studies, organized seminars, and acted as a focal point for representatives of indigenous peoples around the world. The WGIP has been drafting a Universal Declaration of Indigenous Rights, which if adopted in its present form, could be a landmark document for indigenous rights. NGOs such as Survival International, Anti-Slavery International, and the Minority Rights Group are heavily involved in the indigenous rights movement. As a symbolic gesture to recognize the rights of indigenous people, the UN has declared 1995-2004 the International Decade of the World's Indigenous People.

Internally Displaced Persons

In recent years a staggering number of people have been forced to leave their homes due to ethnic, religious, and political persecution, human-made disasters, or disruption of law. The world's internally displaced persons (IDPs) population outnumbers the global refugee population. An estimated fifteen million persons have fled across international borders (refugees) whereas at least thirty million persons have fled their homes but cannot or choose not to leave their own countries. International concern about the crisis of IDPs and the inadequate assistance they receive has grown in the last decade.

According to the UN High Commission for Refugees (UNHCR), Africa has approximately sixteen million displaced persons. Sudan, enduring the longest civil war on the continent, has four million displaced persons. Other countries with at least a million displaced include Iraq and Bosnia-Herzegovina.

The definition of IDP has been submitted to the UN Commission on Human Rights as "persons . . . who have been forced to flee their homes or places of habitual residence suddenly or unexpectedly as a result of armed conflict, internal strife, systematic violations of human rights or natural or man-made disasters, and who have not crossed an internationally recognized State border." Thus, IDPs fall beyond the scope of the 1951 Convention on Refugees and the 1967 Protocol.

The Commission on Human Rights is not mandated to protect or assist IDPs although on occasion they have provided help, such as in Afghanistan in 1994 when Pakistan closed the border to fleeing Afghans. The International Committee of the Red Cross (ICRC) and nongovernmental organizations assist IDPs, yet the needs of the displaced are greater than their resources alone. Governments are fundamentally responsible for IDPs but often lack the capacity and will to assist them.

The most pressing human rights concern for IDPs is for their physical safety. IDPs remain in their country and are not specifically protected by law or one humanitarian body. Increasingly, civilians are being deliberately displaced for the purpose of "ethnic cleansing."

In 1992 Dr. Francis Deng was appointed as representative of the UN Secretary-General on the question of IDPs. His investigations show a discrepancy in the way the international community treats IDP and refugee populations for example, in Burundi and Sudan, refugees received superior international protection and assistance. Deng's recommendations include development of legal standards and improvement of physical security for IDPs, particularly for women and children. He suggests that either the commission have an enlarged mandate or that a new UN agency be created to collaborate with organizations working with IDPs.

In 1995 the ICRC held a conference in Geneva to examine the legal protection of IDPs, the cooperation of concerned agencies, and ways to avert population movements in the future. Other concerned parties consider regional solutions. A conference in Egypt in 1992 resulted in the Declaration on the Protection of Refugees and Displaced Persons in the Arab World. In 1996 a seminar on Refugees, Migrants, Displaced and Stateless Persons, held in Nepal by the South Asia Forum for Human Rights, recommended a South Asia Protocol/Charter for protection of such persons.

Human rights are imperative for the security and dignity of internally displaced persons and for their freedom of movement and voluntary return home. Governments, the UN, and concerned agencies must accelerate their coordination to improve the assistance to IDPs, tackle the root causes of displacement, and search for durable solutions, or their survival will continue to be at stake.

Landmines

Landmines are a relatively new but very serious issue for human rights activists, due to their widespread use and indiscriminate nature. Of the several types of landmines; in existence, the type of greatest concern is the antipersonnel landmine. These small explosive devices are scattered over some seventy countries, and they are currently deployed in dozens of armed conflicts around the world. Some of the countries that are most affected by landmines include Nicaragua, Sudan, Afghanistan, Angola, Bosnia-Herzegovina, Cambodia, and Somalia.

Landmines were first developed just after World War I, primarily to defend against the tank, but soon they were designed to explode in response to human contact. Landmine use accelerated rapidly after World War II over 400 million have been deployed including sixty-five million since the 1980 Convention on Conventional Weapons, which was intended to limit the use of landmines. As instruments of warfare, antipersonnel landmines are unique in their repercussions. They are "victim activated" and indiscriminate, so the vast majority of victims are innocent civilians. Landmines cannot recognize any ceasefire agreements and continue to maim unsuspecting people decades after the fighting has stopped or after frontlines have changed. The United Nations has calculated that the average antipersonnel landmine costs between $3 and $30, while the cost of clearing a mine may be as high as $1000. Peace-building activities and the return of displaced peoples are put in jeopardy by uncleared landmines, and victims of landmines are often unable to find employment, provide for their families, go to school, or reintegrate into society.

In response to these problems, nongovernmental organizations (NGOs) such as Handicap International, the Mines Advisory Group, and Norwegian People's Aid have been working on the rehabilitation of victims, mine clearance, and mine awareness programs. Programs for psychosocial assistance as well as physical rehabilitation are in operation in several countries. Expatriate and local teams are being trained in the disposal of landmines, and awareness programs in landmine safety and first aid are aiming to reduce the risk of landmine injuries in the years to come.

In 1997 a study commissioned by the International Committee of the Red Cross (ICRC) to investigate the military effectiveness of antipersonnel landmines was conducted by military experts from the Americas, Europe, Africa, Asia, and the Middle East. One of the major conclusions was that antipersonnel landmines have historically had little or no effect on determining the outcome of a conflict. In fact, employing antipersonnel landmines posed a "risk to one's own forces and the loss of tactical flexibility."

The scale of the problem initiated a worldwide campaign to ban antipersonnel landmines in 1991, launched by human rights and medical organizations. Consequently, in December 1997, 127 states signed the Convention on the Prohibition of the Use, Stockpiling, Production and Transfer of Anti-Personnel Mines and on Their Destruction, also known as the "Ottawa Treaty." While this convention will not immediately end the use of these weapons, it is seen as a positive step toward the eventual eradication of the antipersonnel landmine epidemic.

Medical Neutrality

Medical neutrality is the principle that medical personnel are obliged to provide impartial medical assistance to all victims of a conflict. Questions of access to health care in wartime and of protection for those who provide it are vital human rights concerns and are addressed in a wide variety of human rights instruments.

The obligation to heal without discrimination dates back to the Hippocratic Oath (fourth century BC). Physicians throughout history have been considered to have special skills that demand respect.

The context of war has required not only that medical personnel honour neutrality in the provision of treatment, but that combatants honour the independence and neutrality of care providers.

The Geneva Conventions, a series of international treaties first conceived in 1864, require that all war-wounded should receive care and that medical services should be provided without reprisal by belligerents. The protocols extend protection to civilians affected by armed conflict. Protocol II, Article 9 stipulates that "medical and religious personnel shall be respected and protected and shall be granted all available help for the performance of their duties."

Medical neutrality, as defined in the Geneva Conventions of 1949 and their Additional Protocols of 1977, is particularly relevant today as it is flagrantly violated worldwide. Many states are engaged in conflicts whose actors abuse medical personnel and civilians: hospitals are bombed, doctors and nurses are threatened, coerced, or killed, and health care is given prejudicially.

Medical personnel and independent humanitarian organizations that provide medical assistance in war zones such as the International Committee of the Red Cross (ICRC) and *Medecins sans Frontieres* (MSF, known in the United States as Doctors without Borders) are constantly challenged by violations of medical neutrality. In Kabul, Afghanistan, in 1997, the ICRC, MSF, and other Afghan and expatriate medical personnel protested the denial of health services to women and the restrictions placed on women health workers.

The healthcare workers publicly insisted that medical personnel not be forced to discriminate against women and suspended their services in protest.

Gross violations of medical neutrality have also occurred during the recent war in Chechnya, a republic in the western part of Russia. In 1995 Chechen rebels occupied a functioning hospital, disrupted medical services, killed hostages, and used physicians and patients as human shields. In December 1996 in Chechnya, six International Red Cross field hospital workers were executed in their beds.

Today, violations of medical neutrality are met by strong protests to governments, rebels, and the international community. Medical workers who protest abuses of medical neutrality by suspending services often create the moral dilemma of denying medical attention to some innocent victims of a war. The long-term effect of such sanctions can only be analyzed over time.

A new initiative has been undertaken in an attempt to safeguard medical neutrality. The Johannes Wier Foundation for Health and Human Rights, supported by members of the international medical community, has called for a United Nations Special Rapporteur on medical neutrality. The new rapporteur would monitor medical workers' freedom from arrest and torture as well as patients' access to medical treatment without discrimination on the basis of nationality, religion, or ethnic origin in war zones or situations of political tension. Such a position could put additional pressure on the abusers of medical neutrality to follow laws and could demand accountability for violations.

Police Brutality

Police brutality occurs whenever police officers abuse their power by using excessive force against civilians. The category encompasses acts of violence and acts that violate human dignity, including unjustified police shootings of civilians, beatings and chokings of suspects in custody, and methods of inflicting physical or psychological suffering on detainees. Police brutality is one of the most widely reported human rights abuses; in a recent Amnesty International annual report, more than one hundred nations on five continents were cited for incidents of police brutality. The vast majority of these countries lack effective procedures for investigating individual complaints of police brutality, leading human rights organizations to demand that police forces around the world be held to a higher standard of accountability.

Although the problem of police brutality has undoubtedly

existed for as long as the existence of professional police forces, it was not formally addressed as a human rights issue until relatively recently. In 1979 the United Nations General Assembly adopted a Code of Conduct for Law Enforcement Officials, calling on police to "uphold the human rights of all persons." Limiting the acceptable use of force to the most extreme circumstances, it also explicitly prohibits law enforcement officials from engaging in "any act of torture or other cruel, inhuman or degrading punishment," making no exception for acts committed under orders or under the threat of public emergency. Threats to public safety or national security are frequently used to attempt to justify police brutality. In Turkey, for example, an armed Kurdish insurrection in the east was used to justify extraordinary violence by Turkish police against civilians around the country violence so condoned by the Turkish judicial system that even members of Turkey's Parliament have been the victims of police brutality.

While police brutality may be perceived as a problem primarily in countries with repressive governments, some liberal Western democracies have an equally troubling record of failing to prevent or punish acts of police brutality. In the past decade both Amnesty International and Human Rights Watch have reported significant numbers of complaints about police violence in the United States, particularly violence against members of racial minorities. Beatings, chokings, and the excessive and sometimes fatal use of firearms were frequently reported. Complaints were also raised about the alarming lack of accountability in police departments across the United States, allowing police officers repeatedly accused of human rights abuses to go without punishment and frequently without investigation.

The rage and frustration experienced by communities affected by police brutality was fatally dramatized in 1992 in Los Angeles, when rioters burned parts of Los Angeles in response to a white jury's acquittal of police officers videotaped while beating African American motorist Rodney

King. In another well-publicized brutality case in 1997, police officers in New York City savagely beat Haitian immigrant Abner Louima and subsequently attempted to cover up their actions starkly illustrating the warnings of several human rights organizations who had reported increasing incidents of police brutality during Mayor Rudolph Guiliani's administration. While activists in the United States and around the world have had some success in raising awareness of police brutality as a serious human rights issue, it still remains to be seen whether experiments to increase police accountability, like those now taking place in cities like New York and Los Angeles, will be able to effectively address the problem.

Freedom of Press

The right to free access of information, which is the basis for freedom of the press, is a universally accepted human right. However, many states place restrictions on the press, ranging from limitations of journalistic independence to publication licensing laws. Every week, journalists, editors, and publishers are threatened, harassed, attacked, banned, imprisoned, and killed.

Restrictions on the press are not new. They were written into state constitutions long ago, such as in the Bangladesh constitution of 1861. Those who most vigorously uphold the rights of the press are often the press themselves. In 1948 the World Association of Newspapers began defending and promoting press freedom. Organizations such as the U.S.-based Committee to Protect Journalists (CPJ) and the France-based *Reporters sans Frontiers* (RSF) were created in the 1980s to monitor cases of restrictions on the press and to campaign on behalf of journalists in danger. Freedom of the press was permanently enshrined in human rights law by Article 19 of the Universal Declaration of Human Rights.

Many state constitutions and even the Universal Declaration contain limitations of rights and freedoms (e.g., in the interest of "national unity," "morality," or "public order"). Some argue that restrictions of the press during times of civil disorder or war are justified, such as during the war in the former Yugoslavia in the early 1990s. Although there are problems in the interpretation of what specifically constitutes a threat to public order, there are clear examples of when "the press" should be restricted in the defense of human rights for others. For example, in Rwanda in 1994, the media was used openly and extensively to call for genocide of Tutsis and moderate Hutus.

Restrictions on the press and crimes against journalists are extremely common, particularly in nondemocratic states. Currently, Nigeria, Colombia, Burma, Ethiopia, and Peru are some of the worst violators of journalists' rights and press freedom. Restriction on the press in democratic states such as the United States and England exist but are far less prevalent. According to the CPJ, at least twenty-six journalists were murdered in fourteen countries in 1997, and 129 journalists were imprisoned in twenty-four countries because of their work. According to CPJ's Executive Director William Orme, in politically troubled nations the independent press frequently becomes the *de facto* opposition to government.

Another organization promoting freedom of expression is the British group, Article 19, which takes its name from Article 19 of the Universal Declaration. Article 19 and more than thirty other organizations are part of International Freedom of Expression Exchange (IFEX) which links groups worldwide, such as Russia's Glasnost Defense Foundation and the Pacific Islands News Association. IFEX's Action Alert Network produces rapid action updates on international press freedom violations in order to effect change.

A hopeful case amidst the many tragic cases of violations of press freedom is the August 1998 amnesty of prominent dissident Doan Viet Hoat, following a major campaign for his release. A sixty-four year old Vietnamese academic and journalist, he was sentenced in 1990 to fifteen years imprisonment for publishing an underground magazine, *Dien Dan Tu Do* (Freedom Forum). His release illustrates the influence of international pressure.

Standing firmly against restrictions on press are members of the press who courageously and continuously defend their right to seek and publish information despite risks. Their colleagues and human rights organizations together act to protect them and the human right to free information.

Prisoners

Broadly speaking, there are three main types of prisoners: common law prisoners, political prisoners, and prisoners of war. Common prisoners are persons detained by the State for having committed a crime against the common law in force in that state, whereas political prisoners have committed offenses aimed against the state or having a political character. Prisoners of war may be defined as combatants who have fallen into the hands of the enemy. Protecting prisoners against ill-treatment and monitoring the conditions of their detention have been important human rights tasks because prisoners are among the most vulnerable groups for potential abuse by authorities.

After the horrors of World War II a new sense of how states must behave *vis-a-vis* their population emerged. Two of the most significant documents to discuss the treatment of prisoners are the Third and Fourth Geneva Conventions of 1949, the former dealing with prisoners of war, and the latter with the civilian population. (Civilian internees enjoy a similar protection to that granted to prisoners of war.) Many subsequent human rights instruments though not solely adopted for the protection of prisoners also provide fundamental safeguards for their treatment. Torture and other forms of ill-treatment are prohibited, as are extrajudicial executions, disappearances, and other misconduct that can particularly affect prisoners.

There are many additional guidelines related to the

rights of prisoners or detainees. For example, the Standard Minimum Rules for the Treatment of Prisoners adopted in 1955 by the First United Nations Congress on the Prevention of Crime and Treatment of the Offenders deal solely with the conditions of detention, emphasizing rehabilitation and restraint of a prisoner rather than retribution and deterrence. This document has been followed by many others, notably the Body of Principles for the Protection of all Persons under Any Form of Detention or Imprisonment. This Body of Principles tries to protect all detainees from abuses such as arbitrary detention, coercive interrogation, and other ill-treatment. The focus is on safeguarding the physical safety of detainees, on the importance of access to the outside world, and on independent supervision of the conditions of detention.

The UN Commission on Human Rights as well as the Sub-Commission on Prevention of Discrimination and Protection of Minorities and its Working Group on the Administration of Justice have been discussing issues related to prisons in general, such as the conditions of detention, judicial guarantees like habeas corpus procedures, and the death penalty, among many others. The International Committee of the Red Cross intervenes on behalf of prisoners of war and interned civilians. The ICRC visits prisoners and, if necessary, tries to convince the authorities to fully respect the rights granted by the Geneva Conventions of 1949. There are also many non-governmental organizations working in the field for the protection of prisoners. For example, prisoners are a major focus of Amnesty International, which monitors and denounces abuses committed by authorities.

Unfortunately, it is never enough. The two components of the protection of prisoners (treatment and material conditions of detention) still require a lot of thought and action. In this respect an interesting related issue is the privatization of prisons, which is taking place around the world. Prisoner advocates have expressed concern about the possible consequences this may have on the conditions of detention and the treatment of prisoners. The UN Sub-Commission on Prevention of Discrimination and Protection of Minorities has decided to study this question in the future.

Rape

Rape is sexual intercourse achieved by the use of force or coercion and without the victim's consent. Its targets are overwhelmingly female. Rape has only recently come to be recognized as a human rights issue of international concern, as it has been used as an instrument of terror and genocide in conflicts in Rwanda and the former Yugoslavia.

Rape is committed in times of peace and war, in private homes and in public institutions. Rape perpetrated in wartime has been a violation of international law since the earliest codification of the laws of warfare. However, like peacetime rape, it is an often overlooked crime. For example, the Charter of the International Military Tribunals at Nuremberg after World War II did not mention rape as a crime against humanity.

The recent conflict in the former Yugoslavia has spotlighted rape as a deliberate military tactic; it is estimated that twenty thousand to fifty thousand women were victims of systematic rape in that war. For the first time, the International Criminal Tribunals for Rwanda and the former Yugoslavia have said they will address rape as a human rights violation. This region is not particularly unique, however; in recent years mass rapes in military conflict have been reported in Afghanistan, Bangladesh, Burundi, Cambodia, Liberia, Peru, Rwanda, Somalia, and Uganda.

Judicial systems deal with rape in a variety of ways. Until recently in most countries, it was legally impossible for a husband to rape his wife. Now the majority of countries technically outlaw marital rape; however, the laws are only enforced in a handful of states. In some countries a woman who reports being raped can be jailed herself for committing adultery. In other situations one or two eyewitnesses are required in order to prosecute a rapist. Under some legal systems a rapist is only held responsible if the woman becomes pregnant; often he may escape prosecution if he marries his victim. Women are also particularly vulnerable to rape when they are incarcerated and the word of a convict is rarely believed over that of her jailer.

Rape is one of the world's most underreported crimes. It is estimated that in some parts of the world fewer than five percent of rapes are reported. It is also believed that in a majority of cases the rapist is known to the victim and that many of the victims of rape are children and adolescents. International enactments against rape have struggled to address the issue. Most mentions of rape in war categorize it as a crime against honour. Whose honour–the victim's, her family's, or her country's–is not clear. In virtually no setting is rape understood as a crime based on gender. Even the Convention on the Elimination of All Forms of Discrimination Against Women does not highlight rape as a gender-based hate crime. Recently, however, international law has begun to recognize rape as a crime committed because of the victim's gender.

Although human rights treaties generally do not address rape directly, rape may be analyzed as a human rights violation under existing laws. Most often, rape is defined as part of a genocide campaign, torture, a war crime, or a crime against humanity. The establishment of an International Criminal Court may provide long-needed protection for victims of rape.

Self-Determination

Self-determination is one of the most controversial contemporary human rights issues. While the fundamental principle of self-determination, which declares the right of peoples to choose their leaders and paths of development, is the first article of the two UN Covenants, application of the right is selective and the definition disputed. Self-determination has been described as "one of most confused expressions in the lexicon of international law." Some legal scholars argue that self-determination is mythical and exists as a principle but not a legal right, whereas others say it has achieved historical legitimacy over the last half-century.

The origin of self-determination can be traced to the 1776 American Declaration of Independence and the 1789 French Declaration of the Rights of Man and the Citizen. Both declarations articulated the inherent right of peoples to choose their own government or form of government. V. I. Lenin of the then-USSR proclaimed annexation of territories to be a violation of the "self-determination of peoples" and Woodrow Wilson, U.S. president during World War I, said the principle of self-determination is an element of peace.

After World War II the concept of self determination was applied in the context of the decolonization process. In 1960 the UN General Assembly adopted its Declaration on the Granting of Independence to Colonial Countries and Peoples (Resolution 1514), stating that by virtue of their right to self-determination, all peoples could "freely determine their political status and freely pursue their economic, social and cultural development." Under these principles, for example, Angola and Mozambique gained their independence from Portugal in 1975.

Collective self-determination has come to imply the rights of the majority to determine their government and development. Today, governments rarely recognize the right to self-determination because in almost all cases it is minority groups who seek it. Indigenous peoples and ethnic minorities for example in East Timor or in the western Sahara suffer because of the lack of self-determination, even though the international community acknowledges that many continue to live under colonialism.

Present day struggles for self-determination receive little international legal support even if the moral and political cases are clear. Eritrea, once considered an integral part of the sovereign state of Ethiopia, recently won its independence, but with a dearth of assistance from the international community. Tibetans, whose country has been occupied by China since 1959, fight for self-determination with weak support from only some governments in the UN.

In Australia, the Aboriginal peoples are making small gains in their battle against substandard social and economic conditions and for indigenous ownership of land. The Aboriginal Land Rights Act passed in 1976, giving them inalienable freehold title to Aboriginal reserves in the Northern Territory. Their efforts toward cultural and economic survival and to make their own decisions on land and resources continue.

Critics of the principle of self-determination express concern about the potential creation of a world of states drawn upon ethnically based lines. However, such a fear does not overshadow the reality of human rights violations of dominated peoples and disregard for the principle of self-determination. Whether colonized peoples seek full independence, autonomy, or the restoration of rights over territory, cultural life, and resources, self-determination is considered the base for the enjoyment of all other human rights and fundamental freedoms.

Sexual Minorities

The term "sexual minorities" refers to the concept of sexual orientation-homosexuality, bisexuality, and transexuality. The term may also be interpreted to address certain practices, such as cross dressing. Human rights issues of concern to sexual minorities vary widely: in some nations, such as the United States, primary concerns include hate crimes, workplace discrimination, and the right to marry. In other nations, sexual minorities struggle for the legal right to simply exist. Although it is estimated that ten to twenty percent of the world's population falls into the category, no UN human rights instrument currently addresses the issue of sexual orientation.

Prior to World War II, issues relating to sexual minorities were virtually not discussed, although homosexuals were among those targeted for extermination by the Nazis. In the last fifty years lesbian and gay human rights organizations have become involved in international human rights law, seeking protection, for example, under Articles 2, 7, and 12 of the Universal Declaration of Human Rights. Even so, when lesbian and gay organizations were accredited to participate in the UN World Conference on Human Rights in 1993, it was the first time the UN had invited the participation of groups representing sexual minorities.

Around the world, sexual minorities face discrimination in a variety of arenas. In several Asian countries, for example, homosexual sex is illegal and may result in arrest and imprisonment. According to Amnesty International, sentences for Iranian women convicted of lesbianism include "cleaving in two halves lengthwise, pushing off a cliff, or stoning to death." In Zimbabwe a gay rights exhibit was banned from a 1995 book fair in Harare by the government: when there were protests, President Robert Mugabe declared that homosexuals had no rights. In 1997 an official with the African Reformed Church in Zimbabwe called for homosexuals to be publicly flogged, and that same year Amnesty International undertook the cause of Mariana Cetiner, a prisoner of conscience being held in Romania because she was a lesbian.

Sexual minorities in the United States face discrimination as well; numerous states have anti-gay laws on the books, and in a majority of states, employees can be fired because of their sexual orientation. When a popular U.S. television star, Ellen Degeneres, acknowledged her lesbianism, she was denounced by several religious organizations, and some companies withdrew sponsorship of her show. In 1998 the voters of the state of Maine repealed a gay rights law that had been passed by the legislature.

Also in 1998 a young student at the University of Wyoming was tortured and murdered because he was gay.

Discrimination against sexual minorities is rarely discussed in international forums. However, in 1994, the UN Commission on Crime Prevention and Criminal Justice recommended the decriminalization of homosexual activities. Also in 1994, in the case of *Toonen v. Australia*, the UN Human Rights Committee found that the prohibition of discrimination on the basis of sex, as contained in the International Covenant on Civil and Political Rights, includes sexual orientation. At the Fourth World Conference on Women in 1995, delegates considered including sexual orientation as a basis of discrimination in the Platform of Action. Although sexual orientation was ultimately not included, the conference marked one of the first protracted discussions of the issue on an international stage. The High Commissioner for Refugees has also held that a "social group," one of the bases for political persecution, includes lesbians and gay men.

Debate over sexual orientation is held on many levels religious and cultural, as well as international. With such a variety of local regulations affecting sexual minorities, the leadership of the international community becomes especially important. United Nations agencies have begun to recognize discrimination based on sexual orientation, as have nongovernmental organizations such as Amnesty International. Although progress is slow, promising steps have been made in recent years.

Slavery

Slavery, the ownership of one person by another, was one of the very first human rights issues to be regulated through international law. In the late twentieth century the definition of slavery has evolved to include a variety of slavery-related practices, including debt bondage, serfdom, child indenture, and marital and sexual bondage.

During the Congress of Vienna in 1815, it was declared that slavery was repugnant to the values of the civilized international community. Since then, numerous instruments as well as national laws have prohibited slavery. In 1926 the Slavery Convention defined slavery as "the status or condition of a person over whom any or all of the powers attaching to the right of ownership are exercised" (Article 1.1). The same convention also prohibits slave trade. Slavery is illegal in every corner of the world. In 1980 Mauritania was the last nation to criminalize the practice, although it should be noted that in recent years Mauritania (along with the Sudan) has come under fierce criticism by the international community for turning a blind eye to the continued existence of slavery.

The slave trade of black Africans to the Americas until the nineteenth century is probably the most evident and dramatic example of slavery, but it is not the only one. For example, "comfort women" used by the Japanese military during World War II were victims of sexual slavery. And in 1998 the UN Commission on Human Rights condemned the enslavement of children, particularly by the Lord's Resistance Army in Northern Uganda.

The actions undertaken against slavery are manifold. First, they have taken the form of conventions and international agreements. The Universal Declaration of Human Rights states that "[n]o one shall be held in slavery or servitude; slavery and the slave trade shall be prohibited in all their forms." This prohibition is also present in the International Covenant on Civil and Political Rights (Article 8.1), the European Convention for the Protection of Human Rights and Fundamental Freedoms (Article 4), and the American Convention on Human Rights (Article 6). The International Labour Organization has two noteworthy conventions on this subject: the Convention Concerning Forced or Compulsory Labour of 1930 and the Convention Concerning the Abolition of Forced Labour of 1957. More recently, slavery has been included as a crime against humanity and a war crime under the statute of the new International Criminal Court.

The United Nations has undertaken several discussions and studies on the issue, such as the 1982 UN Commission on Human Rights Report of Benjamin Whittaker. Various organs and forums deal specifically with the topic of slavery, such as the Independent Expert on the Sale of Children and the Working Group on Contemporary Forms of Slavery. The Working Group is a good indicator of the important current issues related to slavery. The following topics are under discussion: systematic rape; sexual slavery and slavery like practices during armed conflict; traffic in persons and exploitation of others; trans-border traffic in women and girls for sexual exploitation; the role of corruption in the perpetuation of slavery and slavery like practices; misuse of the Internet for the purpose of sexual exploitation; child domestic workers and child labour; debt bondage and bonded labour; and the sale of children for prostitution and pornography.

Torture

Torture the infliction of severe physical and/or psychological pain for purposes such as coercion, punishment, or gaining information is universally condemned as a violation of fundamental human rights. Numerous, widely accepted international instruments prohibit the practice, including the International Covenant on Civil and Political Rights, the American Convention on Human Rights, the European Convention for the Protection of Human Rights and Fundamental Freedoms, the Geneva Conventions of 1949, and many others.

The use of torture, especially during interrogations, has been widespread, both historically and geographically. Ancient Greeks were known to have tortured their slaves for information, and the practice has continued throughout history most notably during papal inquisitions, when Pope

Innocent IV sanctioned the torturing of heretics in 1252. Torture has been practiced for different purposes frequently as a method of gathering information or proof, but also as a punishment or as a way of suppressing political opposition and in different contexts (in times of armed conflict, for example). In the twentieth century torture methods have gone beyond the physical and into the realm of the psychological, including humiliation and threats, sleep deprivation, and the use of pharmacological agents.

Many different mechanisms exist to combat such practices. The United Nations Committee Against Torture, created by the 1984 Convention, has authority to investigate situations that appear to reveal the existence of a systematic practice of torture in a state. One of the challenges ahead for this organ is to clarify the scope of the definition of torture in the 1984 Convention. There is also a possible overlapping between the work of the Committee and the Special Rapporteur on Torture appointed by the UN Commission on Human Rights. There also exists a Working Group on an Optional Protocol to the Convention Against Torture, working to create a preventive system of periodic visits to places of detention. Non-governmental organizations like Amnesty International and the World Organization Against Torture help focus international attention on violations and offer assistance to victims. Finally, different regional judiciary (the European and Inter-American Courts of Human Rights) or quasi-judiciary organs (the Inter-American Commission on Human Rights and the European Commission on Human Rights) make an important contribution by developing case law in the fields of human rights.

For instance, the European Court of Human Rights declared the combination of five techniques used by the British authorities during the interrogation of persons in Northern Ireland to be torture: forcing detainees to stand for periods of some hours in a "stress position," leaning against a wall; putting black hoods over the detainees' heads at all times except during interrogation; holding detainees pending interrogation in a room where there was a continuous loud hissing noise; depriving detainees of sleep pending interrogation; and subjecting detainees to a reduced diet during the period of detention.

Traffic in Women and Girls

Traffic in women and girls refers to the practice of abducting, delivering, or selling women and girls across international borders. Most often, they are forced into prostitution; however, the mail-order bride industry and forcible exportation of women and girls to work in foreign countries are also common. The United Nations estimates that four million girls and women are trafficked internationally every year. Human rights activists are concerned not only with the sale of human beings a blatant human rights violation but also with the often-abusive treatment of the women and girls after the sale has occurred.

The first international agreement banning the traffic of women for "immoral purposes" went into effect in 1912. In 1950 the Convention for the Suppression of the Traffic in Persons and the Exploitation of the Prostitution of Others came into effect. Both the Convention on the Elimination of All Forms of Discrimination Against Women and the Convention on the Rights of the Child forbid trafficking.

Nonetheless, in recent years trafficking in women and girls has increased and become more organized than ever before. A major cause of the expansion of the industry is the growth of sex tourism. Emerging nations rely on tourism to stimulate their economic growth. One of the most lucrative kinds of tourism consists of men from rich nations travelling to poorer nations to take advantage of the sex business, in which young girls are purchased from their families for use as prostitutes. Sexism and racism intertwine to support sex tourism; sexism that devalues women in general and racism that implies that women in certain cultures are more subservient and available than in others.

Another kind of trafficking is the mail order bride industry. Here, brokers in poor countries recruit women to marry men in richer countries. Although some of these marriages work out, more often they do not. Many of the women who do marry are mistreated by their husbands, again supported by racism and sexism. Often, husbands will abandon their wives after a short period of time, leaving them without money in a strange country, possibly illegally. Or, the broker may in reality be procuring women for prostitution, and there never was a husband waiting at all.

Trafficking in women and children is sometimes not for an overtly sexual purpose. Instead, women and children from poor countries are sent to richer nations to work as maids, nannies, and nurses. Often they are sexually abused; if not, they are usually subjected to inhumane working conditions. They may be literally imprisoned in their employer's home, completely isolated and without means of escape. They may be overworked and physically abused by their employers, or the job offers may be, once again, a ruse for obtaining prostitutes.

Women and children are obtained by traffickers in a variety of ways. In impoverished nations, girls may be sold by their parents. In some cases, women and children are kidnapped or, when recruiters misrepresent the jobs available in other countries, the women may volunteer to go.

Currently, a variety of organizations (e.g., Human Rights Watch) are addressing the trafficking issue. Some are encouraging the United Nations to implement treaties that address sexual exploitation as a violation of human rights. Some groups are targeting sex tourism, while others rescue and rehabilitate women and children who have been abused. All are concerned that existing laws be enforced effectively.

3

Modern Human Rights Movement

Until the atrocities committed by the Axis states (Germany, Italy, and Japan) in World War II fundamentally altered the climate of interstate discourse, virtually all states were unwilling to allow outsiders to critique the treatment of their citizens. Leaders of most states considered the handling of rebels, prisoners, the destitute, the handicapped, women, and children purely an internal matter governed by history, religion, and tradition. The legacy of that parochialism allowed totalitarian states to abridge the human rights of their and other state' citizens on an enormous scale. Few totalitarian dictators ever believed that they would receive their comeuppance, for as Stalin scoffed, "How many [military] divisions does the Pope have?"

Changed attitudes concerning human rights following World War II suddenly allowed international public scrutiny of virtually all countries, coupled with virtually instantaneous sharing of rights data via radio, wire services, and then television. The result was an explosion of information on human rights violations, which ignited interest on the part of ordinary citizens who could now unite together to effect change. The human rights movement was, thus, born.

In this climate the United Nations was created. Its charter included requirements that conventions and declarations to protect human rights be enacted, which led to the establishment of the United Nations Commission on Human Rights, chaired by Eleanor Roosevelt. Two years later, after considerable negotiation and compromise, the Universal Declaration of Human Rights (UDHR) was approved by the General Assembly on December 10, 1948 with a vote of forty-eight in favour, zero against, and eight abstentions, including South Africa, Saudi Arabia, and the Soviet Union.

The promise and the deficiencies of the Universal Declaration were the additional impetus needed to help build a movement. Because the declaration was not a legally binding international document, it could only cajole and inspire states, rather than command their obedience, even to "universal" standards. The effort to implement the declaration took some twenty years and tens of thousands of individuals; finally the draft texts of two key treaties were accepted by the General Assembly. Another ten years passed before the International Covenant on Civil and Political Rights and the International Covenant on Economic, Social, and Cultural Rights became operational in 1976. During that process, ordinary citizens learned that states move slowly, but worldwide bodies can inch forward at a glacial pace. Into that near vacuum of policy enforcement, groups of citizens organized to expose abuses, shame perpetrators, and educate the public.

Some of these NGOs worked hard to influence the United Nations, glacial though its progress was. Several other important international documents were shepherded through the UN system between 1948 and 1976, notably declarations that further refined the Universal Declaration. Although most consider declarations in the UN context vital in clearly understanding treaty documents (or conventions), their lack of enforcement mechanisms often limits their usefulness until, or if, a companion treaty follows. In one example to the contrary, the 1975 Declaration on the

Protection of All Persons from Being Subjected to Torture and Other Cruel, Inhuman, or Degrading Treatment or Punishment, was a success largely due to the work of one NGO, Amnesty International. Because the twelve articles in the torture declaration offered practical and clear-cut advice for states in evaluating their employees, they also aided aggrieved citizens and human rights movements in proving their cases.

Perhaps the most successful human rights efforts occurred in the wake of the 1975 Helsinki Accords (see below), when Amnesty International's anti torture efforts, including the torture declaration and convention and worldwide letter-writing campaigns by legal, religious, medical, and psychiatric bodies, dramatically influenced the lives of persons incarcerated for their beliefs. Well-organized and funded NGOs can move proverbial mountains. The efforts of Amnesty International were instrumental in the passage of the follow-on 1984 UN convention on torture, which reinforced the declaration and was an important enforcement step. Amnesty International also directly influenced the passage of other subsequent declarations and led to other treaties affecting the treatment of incarcerated persons worldwide. These efforts radically changed the environment for persons accused of crimes and even helped facilitate the campaigns of the 1980s and 1990s that liberated many celebrated prisoners. Other NGOs followed, such as Doctors Without Borders, Human Rights Watch, and many others so much so that some of the most influential constituents in the movement are NGOs working alongside international and individual government organs.

History of the Human Rights Movement

In the 1950s and 1960s the Soviets repeatedly called for a European security conference, hoping to legitimate its control over the states of East and Central Europe, now firmly lodged behind the Soviet's "Iron Curtain." When the West finally agreed to such a conference, which opened in 1972, it did so only if human and economic rights were added to the discussions and only if the United States and Canada were full participants also. The result of this conference, the Helsinki Accords (officially the Final Act of the Helsinki Meeting of the Conference on Security and Cooperation in Europe, or CSCE), was signed in 1975 by all European and North American states (except Albania). It added dramatic impetus to the successes of NGO efforts on behalf of human rights.

When the Helsinki Accords were published and disseminated behind the Iron Curtain, Helsinki monitoring groups sprang up, arguing that their governments must implement the Accords. These groups were brutally attacked in the Soviet Union and in Czechoslovakia especially, although they also received adverse notice elsewhere in the rest of the bloc. This negative response only heightened Western concerns, and in a series of review conferences between East and West, the East was ultimately so embarrassed and harassed that substantial change began to occur.

After 1985, with the rise of Mikhail Gorbachev in the Soviet Union, the USSR increasingly accepted the humanitarian and human rights principles articulated in Basket Three of the Helsinki Accords. Once the East and Central European revolutions of 1989 occurred, Basket Three offered a standard of behaviour for the reform regimes that followed. At the 1990 Helsinki follow-up meeting in Copenhagen, all of the newly established European states unanimously endorsed multiparty democracy, political pluralism, independent judiciaries, special protection for minority groups, and the separation of the state from free political parties.

This all occurred as an exercise in diplomacy. Not only did the accords lack any "divisions," as Stalin put it, but they had no charter, no budget, and no secretariat. They operated with ad hoc support from the foreign ministries of member states, augmented by a huge NGO community and the world's press. At a time when progress on destabilizing arms control issues loomed large, the success that this diplomatic instrument offered in East-West relations was impressive. Without the accords, the transformation of East and Central Europe, as well as the USSR, would likely not have come so soon or so peacefully.

A Case Study in Human Rights Policy: The Carter Administration

Ever since the founding of America its political elite has grappled with the classic debate over isolation versus engagement in great power politics. Coupled with that debate in the twentieth century has come the struggle over to what degree morality must dictate foreign policy. Few contemporary statesmen, or indeed politicians, adhere to pure idealism, which focuses on morality as the only or primary calculations of the national interest. Similarly, few are whole-hearted supporters of realism, which flouts morality in favour of a pure pursuit of realpolitik, or national interest. Nevertheless, less principled leaders and states use realism as their prime paradigm in directing their nation's conduct, and to engage and defeat them states espousing higher principles must also then pursue realism in foreign affairs.

At the center of the United States' first human-rights-oriented foreign policy effort since World War II after its relative disengagement during the 1950s and part of the 1960s the Carter administration grappled with the trade-off between geopolitics and human rights. Although the Carter administration used virtually all means at its disposal to influence states accused of human rights violations, it was caught up in the reality of state politics, even within its own administration, by practitioners of subtly different persuasions. The superpower rivalry, arms control issues, the grain trade, regional conflagrations, the Soviet invasion of Afghanistan, global energy policies, conflicts with traditional allies, the hostage crisis in Iran [5] and immigration policy all deeply affected President Jimmy Carter's hopes for human rights influence. Nevertheless, because Carter's political emphasis struck a chord with deep-seated American values, it helped heal the bitterness left over from the Vietnam War in the American body politic, just as it added immeasurably to the lives of millions worldwide.

Critics, however, accused the Carter administration of inconsistency, particularly with regard to the implementation, of lack thereof, of stiff responses to human rights violations in states of importance to the United States that were dictated by realism. Similarly, President Carter's policies toward right-wing dictatorships were sometimes criticized for being too harsh, just as he was maligned by many human rights bodies for being too lenient with China and the Shah's regime in Iran. Those who did not understand America's twin poles of isolationism and engagement and those who scoffed at the policy trade-off between idealism and realism in foreign policy saw these apparent zigzags in policy as ripe for criticism.

The high profile of President Carter's efforts internationally occasioned skepticism and active resistance. When the United States sponsored a resolution "calling on the United Nations to appoint a High Commissioner for Human Rights," it was defeated sixty-two to fort-nine, with twenty-one abstentions. The swing votes leading to its defeat came from the developing world and Communist states.

Nevertheless, in the light of intervening years, it seems clear that President Carter's emphasis on human rights as a key priority in geopolitics has reverberated in a salutary fashion around the world. The key issue for him and for subsequent presidents and world leaders is always the question of political will.

Two Concepts of Foreign Policy

In the international human rights context, President Carter is the best example of an idealist in American foreign policy. Idealists argue that the pursuit of morality in foreign policy is compatible with national security concerns. They also argue that America's leadership role in the world is so vital that it must set the very highest standards so that America and its allies can help influence a more peaceful and just world.

On the other end of the spectrum is Hans J. Morgenthau, author of *Politics Among Nations* and founder of the realist school. He argued that the choice for leaders is not between the national interest and moral principles, but rather between moral principles divorced from political reality and moral principles derived from political reality. America's senior foreign policy elites have tended to be most sympathetic to the realist school of foreign policy. In recent years, President Richard M. Nixon and his Secretary of State Henry Kissinger have evidenced it, as has President Carter's National Security Adviser Zbigniew Brzezinski, President George Bush, and Secretary of State George Shultz.

United States needs to do more than make declarations and to provide free transport for fleeing dictators. . . . The U.S. government has leverage to use if it chooses to use it. *It has the power to persuade governments*".

Ongoing Controversies in the Human Rights Movement

Although international consensus on the importance of human rights has increased in the last fifty years, the questions raised during the formation of the movement are far from answered.

Human Rights as Western Imperial Legacy

In the contest for rights the West was dealt a strong hand. Not only was there a firm belief in the value and efficacy of inherited institutions, but the West supported a substantial and growing population, it maintained fleets of trading and warships, and it possessed the world's most powerful weapons and largest armies, along with the most efficient network of transport and communications. By the end of the nineteenth century, Western political and economic clout extended far beyond European settlement. By 1914 almost all of Africa, Latin America, south and south-east Asia, and Oceania had come under European or American political control. Farms, mines, and plantations were opened in many largely virgin areas, often at places remote from Western or any other sort of civilization. New products like tea, rubber, nickel, and oil mingled together with old ones like gold and diamonds; new two-way commercial ventures were established (like cotton and cloth in India and Egypt); and traders, missionaries, and settlers moved into every area previously considered inaccessible.

These efforts by colonial powers and the peoples and commodities who moved under their imprimatur, whether loose or deliberate fundamentally altered the older distributions of populations, cultures, and orientations in the world. Mountain barriers, oceans, and even parched and windswept plains were no longer sufficient to halt the Western advance, and few militaries were able but to stall the march of Westerners and their ideals, religion, trade, and technology.

As such, human rights philosophy and the subsequent movement in support of it flowered in the West and dispersed along old lines of influence around the globe. Nevertheless, only in Western democratic societies, with their shared philosophies and historical and economic development, does the support for human rights run as deeply in philosophy, society, and law. The Western emphasis is centered on the liberty of the person. Not only does he or she have the right to hold and express individual intellectual and religious beliefs, but he or she also possesses the right to physical security. By contrast, other traditions–Asian, African, Islamic, and to a lesser extent Latin lack the same emphasis on individual political rights. Illustrative of these differences is the actual language of the Universal Declaration, which devotes only three of its thirty articles to economic rights, the emphasis of which is more common in more traditional, communal societies. Similarly, socialist states, irrespective of the region, also lack an emphasis on civil rights, emphasizing group and economic rights instead.

Cultural Differences and Human Rights

> *"The debate on human rights assumes that in spite of the differences that characterize the spectrum of world cultures, political conduct can be conceptualized by certain common norms and attitudes. In the modern global system, Westerners have concentrated on discovering common denominators rooted in Judeo Christian traditions and from which a calculus of human rights would emerge."*

Latin America

The Central and South American countries that compose Latin America were settled in the modern age primarily by the Spanish and Portuguese. Over the intervening centuries these Europeans blended with indigenous Indian tribes to produce an ethno-racial group that was augmented by the arrival of African slaves, other Europeans, Asians, and North Americans. As such, the peoples are a polyglot, but the dominant political culture is still Western, albeit with a Latin flavour.

In the period after World War II, an aversion to political rights and free and fair elections was justified (by some governments) by the threat of Communism. The argument that human rights should be held in abeyance until after development also continued to apply. Many assessments suggest that both justifications were convenient excuses needed to justify a military junta or a coup.

Indeed, the legitimacy of a regime is a question that has plagued many Latin American countries for some time. This problem is particularly acute when otherwise apolitical militaries cannot meet their oaths to preserve, protect, and support a civilian regime that has ceased to exist through turmoil, anarchy, or disputed elections. The Latin political culture in the post-World War II period became so chaotic at times that military intervention became legitimate, because the military was popularly viewed by the citizenry as their final guardian of popular sovereignty.

However, with the worldwide growth in pluralism in the 1980s and 1990s, much of Latin America also enjoyed a return to civilian rule as well as greater popular sovereignty and strengthened commitment to human rights issues.

> *"parochial view of human rights that excludes the cultural realities and present existential conditions of Third World societies. What has occurred is the reshaping of politics to accommodate various theories of political behaviour gleaned from Western traditions."*

Abdul Aziz said

> *At the root of the cultural differences concerning rights was the fundamental dichotomy that existed between Western and non-Western societies. Western industrial states have traditionally placed a substantial emphasis on individual rights, with government initially only grudgingly guaranteeing some basic economic support for the least fortunate. By contrast, non-Western traditional societies have tended to meet their needs more communally, stressing reliance on the family and the group. Not yet heavily industrialized, with a majority of the population in agriculture, and with a limited educational base, a marginal climate and/or limited resources, these societies are centered around the clan, the tribe, extended families, and/or local, isolated communities. The group, thus, becomes the defining element of society, not the individual, particularly if the society is on the margin, with scant hope of survival without the entire populace tightly organized.*

When Western views on rights met Eastern, African, and to a lesser extent Latin views, further distinctions emerged. Westerners tend to emphasize individual responsibility for economic and social progress within a broader state economic structure, while many non-Western states find these to be key duties of the state. In the latter, individual political or human rights are clearly communal if considered at all, and of lesser importance.

When these largely African and Asian states became independent of colonial powers in the wake of World War II, little changed for the individual, although as groups the populace became sovereign states. What had traditionally been a set of obligatory responsibilities toward the group now became responsibilities due the state; what rights had been bestowed by the group now became the purview of the state to bestow (or withdraw) as it so wished. As Indira Gandhi of India told *The New York Times* in 1975, "It is not individuals who have rights but states."

Decolonization, Development, and Human Rights

Decolonization and subsequent efforts toward economic development of newly independent nations offer ongoing and fundamental challenges to the human rights movement. In Africa and Asia the British Westminster model employed during colonial rule, which emphasized individual rights, was incorporated into virtually all constitutions during decolonization and has survived largely intact over the decades. Departures from the model tended to be in states with civil upheavals, where authoritarian and/or military leaders scrapped the inherited constitutions of civilian rule. In those states either a one party state was imposed or a military junta ruled. In both cases, political liberties withered on the vine, usually covered by transparent appeals to communal and economic rights that would be respected. Typically, "preventive" detention laws were put in place, freedom of speech, press, and association was restricted, most if not all political parties were outlawed, the judiciary and legislative functions were subsumed under the authoritarian or military rulers, and normally nonpolitical groups such as aid societies, religious bodies, and educational institutions were allowed to exist only if they subsumed themselves under the rulers' control. Soon the promised economic rights disappeared under nationalizations of key industries, with political leaders and their cronies siphoning off the lion's share of the proceeds. The Philippines' Ferdinand Marcos and Zaire's Mobutu Sese Seko were particularly adept at such schemes.

Many authoritarian and military-led states argued that democratic ideals and human rights should be sacrificed in the present and pursued in the future in order to concentrate on economic development. It was argued by many that development would bring economic rights, which in turn would meet the needs for human dignity by emancipating the masses from colonial exploitation and dependence. Julius Nyerere in Tanzania, Sekou Toure in Guinea, and Kwame Nkrumah in Ghana all prominently espoused this argument, winning converts at home and abroad. In like manner, the explosion of Latin military dictatorships of the 1950s through 1980s or the Greek military coup of 1967 justified the removal of personal freedoms in the name of preserving order. When trials of torturers were held following Greece's liberation from the military in 1974, the torturers were not tried for gross abrogation of human rights but merely "misuse of authority," since no law made torture illegal in Greece.

Rights in the postcolonial era tended to be defined with regard to colonialism. Most postcolonial states achieved independence at an early stage of economic development, with low gross domestic products (GDPs), low levels of literacy and savings, little indigenous capital generation, and a population still primarily in agriculture or pastoral pursuits. If the colonial legacy in a state was relatively benign, then the transition to a Western-style concept of rights was generally not seriously challenged. Where the colonial administration was rapacious and the economic impact exploitative, then postcolonial rights tended to be viewed against that prism, with economic concerns paramount, rather than civil concerns celebrating the rights of the individual. In states where the per capita income was exceedingly low, rights came to be assessed as freedom from want and the money needed to educate and clothe children, with something left over for feeble, later years. Medical access, educational access, and free or low-cost land were all far more important than somewhat abstract concepts of political rights.

Indeed, until mass secondary education has become standard and a rising middle class has succeeded sufficiently well that it has something to lose (as began to occur in the West in the eighteenth and nineteenth centuries), most developing societies do not naturally and intimately focus themselves on individual rights. The educated few, government elites, and sometimes the church, as well as the expatriate community, tend to be those most intimately involved in helping protect individual rights until the rising tide of development makes the concept real and vital to the masses.

In that vein it is worth stating something widely observed about developing states in the post-World War II period: support for democratic development is rarely more than skin-deep. Because Western political democracy is not only based upon deep levels of educated participation but upon legal guarantees, it is often dispensed with by authoritarian or military regimes in the developing world. The decades of the 1960s and 1970s were especially worrisome to those who feared sweeping tides of authoritarianism and misery wiping out fledgling democratic governments. One-party states became common in Africa, as charismatic leaders like Sekou Toure, Nyerere, and Nkrumah stamped out political dissent. Nkrumah argued that "the Convention People's Party (CPP) is Ghana and Ghana is the CPP."

Throughout the 1980s and 1990s, participatory democracy or polyarchy, as Robert Dahl coined it to avoid anti U.S. or anti-Western bias began to sweep the globe, first in Latin America and later in key states in Africa and Asia. As these more pluralistic states came to power, so did greater willingness to reinstitute Western notions of rights. The press became freer, dissent opened up, parties blossomed, and conditions for women and children improved.

Problem of Enforceability

The problems of enforcing human rights arise from the multiplicity of instruments, entities, and individual interests at play in the human rights movement. There is no single ideology that defines what human rights are and no monolithic structure that has the jurisdiction to supervise their enforcement.

Although Eleanor Roosevelt, as chair of the Human Rights Commission, stated in 1948 that the Universal Declaration of Human Rights "is not a treaty; it is not an international agreement, it is not and does not purport to be a statement of law or legal obligation," many who worked on the issue clearly hoped that it would go beyond the recommendation format and become the new international norm. They recognized that the declaration format was the best they could hope to achieve in 1948.

Over time the Universal Declaration has come to be regarded as binding upon the signatory states, with many citing Article 6 of the Convention on the Elimination on All Forms of Racial Discrimination, adopted by the General Assembly and put into force in 1969, and the Preamble of the International Covenant on Economic, Social and Cultural Rights of 1966 as having made the declaration binding by reaffirming the declaration's principles. Custom has also reaffirmed the declaration's principles as binding in international law.

Since the Universal Declaration a rapidly growing number of states have incorporated explicit support for human.

Rival Cultural Tradition

The role of government, the state, religion, and the rights of the individual are fundamentally different under Islam from what exists in the West. An Islamic government exists to ensure that the *Shariah* is enforced. In these states God is viewed as the ultimate arbiter and legislator. It is assumed that all, rulers and ruled, are jointly entwined in an enterprise that will promote God's glory. As such, human legislation is far less important than it is in the West, since it is believed that God's wishes are clear and that only relatively minor matters need go before the judges.

According to scholar Abdul Aziz Said, Islamic legal theory "provides no adequate machinery to safeguard individual rights against the state." As a result, various Islamic states, or states with a significant proportion of their populace who are Muslim, have designed a variety of coping strategies. On one end of the spectrum Saudi Arabia applied the *Shariah* fully and literally. By contrast Pakistan has provided for individual rights through a liberal analysis of the oldest sources of Islamic law. Turkey took another tack: since modern Turkey's founding by Kemal Ataturk (1881- 1938), Turkey has guaranteed individual rights in a secular state. Similarly, Egypt has attempted to accommodate both Islam and Christianity in a constitution-based state on the British model. All three of these latter states, along with others, have found the struggle to protect individual liberties along Western lines difficult, given the recent growth of Islamic fundamentalism.

The record of human rights protection in Islamic states is varied. With traditional Islamic codes viewed as losing their utility as safeguards for rights within Islam, and with modern philosophical and state constructs not yet fully accepted, individual rights and their protectors are in turmoil. With divisions in Islam serious enough to fight major conflicts over (such as in Afghanistan and in Iraq) and with continuing hostility and rivalry among sunni, shia, and rival sects (such as the Wahhabis who rule Saudi Arabia), a common agenda for individual rights in Islamic states is not assured.

Like the Judeo-Christian tradition, there is much in Islam that would seem to augur well for the protection of individual dignity. The concept of *dhimmis* promises Christians, Jews, and other groups that an Islamic country is committed to protecting the possibility of existing within an Islamic state. Moreover, the Koran encourages moderate life, without inordinate emphasis on wealth-building: "And thus we have made you a people with moderate virtues in order that you may be a witness to men" (2:143). Islam also fears poverty, for it can lead the poor away from God. Thus, a Muslim expects his or her state to help meet the basics of housing, food, and clothing for all.

Humans are viewed as being created in the image of God and are considered God's representatives (*khalifah*) on earth. Humans are expected to receive certain rights from their God, with individual freedom achieved in perfect subservience to God. Because this type of freedom is individual, and eternal, Muslims don't look for it through public legislation. Rather, an individual is free in Islam until his freedom hinders the community; at that point, the state intervenes. Similarly, the *Shariah* describes rights and freedoms, but they come with obligations towards God and others. The, *Shariah* states that unless obligations are accepted and fulfilled, individuals are not allowed rights. Similarly, without fulfilment of obligations, any claims of freedom from the state are not acceptable.

The twentieth century and its emphasis on human rights has spawned a debate in the Islamic theological in philosophical world concerning rights. One branch of theology, which includes the Asharites, does not weigh human freedom as legitimate. They believe that God's grace determines all. Most Muslim philosophers, however, grant that human freedom exists, all the way back to Avicenna, Averroes, and Farabi, who knew the works of Aristotle, Plato, and the Stoics. However, they did not accept the Greek notion of human freedom but argued instead for freedom for the individual within Islam. This group-based freedom "denies some of the essential Western liberal conceptions of freedom. From the Islamic perspective, the anarchy of liberal individualism cannot be a creative seedbed of culture."

Political freedom, thus, is offered far less latitude than spiritual freedom. Indeed, a constant rivalry exists in Islamic states between temporal rulers and spiritual. In the past the conflict between free will and God's determinism have "produced periods of submission characterized by anarchy and assassination." Political leaders at times are zealous in their support of religious doctrine, while other leaders at other times refuse to do so. As such, religious-based zealotry then induces periods of great conflict between Islamic states and within them, as well as between Islamic countries and their neighbours. The violence that results clearly betrays any latent efforts to protect the sanctity and dignity of the person.

In sum, Islam is at a stage in human history wherein international modes of human rights behaviour are challenging it to change faster than it can without a bitter, internecine struggle for secular, political, and religious power. Islam has yet to accommodate the nation-state within its traditional culture and religion. In order to meet prevailing international norms of human rights, a fundamental social revolution would be required in most Islamic states.

The charters of the Organization of American States (OAS), the Council of Europe, and the Organization of African Unity (OAU) are such examples. This growing organizational entrenchment of liberties gives further support for binding the declaration's principles in international law. These instruments amount to a legal patchwork that lawyers and activists in the international arena must struggle to negotiate.

An enforcement issue indigenous to Western states deals with who holds the upper hand the individual or the state. This rivalry is a two-hundred-year-old issue, but it now has taken on a new dimension with the rise of "welfare states," especially in Western Europe. Starting with the English Petition of Rights and the American and French declarations, more was given to the individual and less was expected of the individual from the state. Over the past two centuries, individual responsibilities and obligations decreased, while individual freedoms grew. By contrast, however, greater rights, prerogatives, and freedoms presumed greater state efforts to protect them. The poor, the landless, children, women, and labourers all needed help in bad times and protection from their rapacious fellows. As such, the state was required to expand its capacity to meet these new needs. Today the state is caught between two poles of human rights advocates. Whenever it intercedes on behalf of one individual or group, it can be accused of denying or neglecting others.

4

Peasant Justice and Human Rights

Introduction

There was a thief who had stolen some radios. We discovered who it was while we were investigating a different robbery. The patrols had organized a commission that was searching house by house. Everyone if they're not guilty accepts that and lets the patrols in. Well, we found the goods, hidden in a wall, covered over with paper. So the patrol detained the thief and brought him before an assembly of the whole community. In an assembly everyone participates, everybody votes. No leader can impose his will. There are different suggestions, we discuss, we vote. In this case they gave the thief a punishment: one week of community labour, helping build a sports field at the school, and one week of night-time patrols. They also gave him five lashes to make him confess, because at first he didn't want to, even though we had all the proof we needed. Before he was punished, he had to swear before all the community, before the organization, that he would not steal again, under threat that next time his punishment would be much worse. And it worked; now he is a loyal member of the community.

To the peasants of the Peruvian Andes, deeply impoverished, long discriminated against, struggling to survive in a largely hostile world, what is the meaning of human rights? During the 1980s, beset by cattle rustling and thievery in general, and in the face of a judicial system that was at best overwhelmingly incompetent and at worst thoroughly corrupt, the peasants of the northern Peruvian department of Cajamarca organized a system of local patrols, or *rondas,* and began to administer justice on their own. By the middle of the decade they had created what was in essence a parallel and informal legal system resolving virtually every kind of local dispute, both civil and criminal. The peasants speak with pride of what they have accomplished. Yet, *ronda* justice, while often effective, quick, fair, and compassionate, echoed some of the abuses of the official system it sought to replace. The *rondas* detained and punished people, with no formal right to do so, and not infrequently coerced confessions. This in turn opened them to attack from their enemies, in particular the state's judiciary itself. The result was the emergence of a discussion within the *rondas* over what the patrols could and could not, or should or should not do, and, in particular, over the use of violence. It is a debate largely dictated by practical pressures: How to avoid repression? But it is one also posed in moral terms: What is proper? In this debate a discourse on human rights has gradually emerged.

For much of the past thirty years, discussions of human rights have been caught up in the debate between universalists and relativists. There is an argument between the advocates of universal rights, who contend that certain rights inhere in all individuals regardless of cultural context, and the cultural relativists, who argue that values are culturally specific and that individualism, freedom of choice, or legal equality are alien and often meaningless.

In recent years the debate has been complicated by the demand for recognition of collective minority rights, in Latin America most often for "indigenous rights." As Rodolfo

Stavenhagen points out, in a context in which indigenous populations have for centuries been exploited, "basic human rights cannot be fully enjoyed, exercised or protected ... if the 'peripheral' rights specific to the groups in question cannot simultaneously be enjoyed, exercised and protected." This demand for minority rights poses the debate over cultural relativism in a new way. Where local indigenous groups are granted limited autonomy to administer their own affairs according to their own values, what happens when their behavior conflicts with national or international norms?

Stated at such levels of generality the debate is seldom constructive. That the origins of the political concept of "human rights" lie in the West and that Western nations have manipulated the concept in self serving ways is unquestionable. Nor can anyone deny that numerous states not only non-Western have sought to mask and legitimate abusive treatment of their citizens behind a discourse of relativism. As Ann-Belinda Preis comments, "At this metageneral level of analysis, almost all arguments become plausible, or equally true or false. One glosses over a multitude of cultural particularities. When the debate is so radically removed from the cultural 'realities' it alleges to speak about, it hardly creates anything but its own impasse."

Yet the idea of human rights has caught on. Whatever its specific content, the notion that there exists something called human rights has become part of political debate of peoples around the world. "In several, formerly 'remote' areas of the world, different human rights discourses have now become a vehicle for the articulation of a wide variety of concerns of different people at different levels of society. Human rights have become 'universalized' as values subject to interpretation, negotiation, and accommodation."

In this chapter I will examine one case by using administration of justice by the peasant patrols of northern Peru of how a discourse on human rights has become a small but real part of discussion among peasants themselves.

This is a discussion in which the idea of individual human rights has acquired meaning precisely because it affects the peasants' immediate lives. I begin with a brief history of the peasant patrols, then outline their administration of justice and some of the problems it has provoked, and conclude with an overview of the debate, still inconclusive, that this has stimulated among the peasants.

Brief History of the *Rondas*

The *rondas* were born because in Chota, near the road from Bambamarca to Tacabamba, there were robberies every night. We would have to remain awake the entire night; we had to bring our cattle into our homes. From my grandparents, first the thieves stole two cows, then three sheep, then they broke into the house and even took their pots and pans. Well, then it occurred to me that the only way to defend ourselves was to organize. So I said to the people: "I think we should organize patrols. While some sleep, others will guard our possessions."

The *rondas campesinas* emerged as an organized communal response to cattle rustling and petty thievery, as "a collective effort to protect individual property." [5] In the department of Cajamarca cattle rustling, which had reached epidemic proportions, was a highly organized profession, involving merchants, Mafia-like gangs, and local agents. The state offered little or no protection; police seldom intervened, courts seldom prosecuted. In response, the peasants of the hamlet of Cuyumalca in December 1976 decided to organize nocturnal patrols to protect their animals and other possessions.

At first, fearful of rustler reprisals or state repression, few communities followed Cuyumalca's example. However, by 1978 the success of the first *rondas* had become obvious in Cuyumalca rustling was controlled and petty thievery greatly reduced, while the *rondas* suffered little repression. By the end of 1980 almost every community in central Cajamarca had organized *rondas*, and in each of the provinces federations had been formed. By the mid-1980s, the *rondas* had spread across most of the northern mountains of Peru.

The core of the patrols were the *grupo de ronda,* the *asamblea,* and the *comité de ronda.* All adult males participated in the *grupos,* units of five to ten peasants who in weekly rotation patrolled fields and trails from evening to sunrise, stopping anyone who appeared suspicious. Policy was made by the *asamblea,* a town meeting in which the entire community participated. To coordinate among *grupos* and manage the day-to-day affairs of the *ronda,* the *asamblea* elected a *comité de ronda,* with a president and directorate. When thefts occurred the *comité* would organize investigations, coordinate via formal notification with the *rondas* of neighbouring communities, and bring suspects before the *asamblea.* Participation in both *grupos* and the *asamblea* was obligatory, and discipline was strict. Peasants who failed to meet their responsibilities were brought before the assembly and punished with fines, additional rotations, or even whippings.

Initially the *rondas* handed thieves over to judicial authorities. However, seldom did the authorities police, government lawyers, or judges prosecute. It was far more common to see the rustlers wandering freely after a few days' detention, a fact that the peasants perceived as evidence of official corruption. The result was a series of dramatic confrontations with both rustlers and state authorities. The decisive event came in 1980, when *ronderos* from dozens of communities in an assembly reputedly attended by more than 5,000 peasants decided to execute a half-dozen rustlers. The 1980 lynchings established the *rondas* as a force to be respected and feared.

But if the *rondas* could punish thieves, they could deal with other problems too. By the mid-1980s the structures the peasants had developed were being used to settle a range of problems, both criminal and civil. These included the classic conflicts that divide peasants (e.g., land ownership, water rights, contracts, debts, inheritances), public order problems (from petty thievery to public drunkenness to interfamily feuds), family conflicts (e.g., adultery, wife beating, child support), and a variety of other difficulties. Earlier most problems would have been taken to the courts, where the cases would have dragged on for years, seldom being solved to the satisfaction of anyone, and then only at great cost. Using the *ronda* was quicker, cheaper, and, in the eyes of most, far more just. Thus by the mid-1980s the *rondas* had assumed the function of what Nora Bonifaz calls "maintaining order." With rustling controlled, "peasant justice" became the core activity of the *rondas.*

The structure of peasant justice was everywhere similar. Anyone could bring a complaint before the *ronda* simply by approaching a member of the *comité.* Where necessary the *comité* would carry out an investigation: examining evidence, questioning witnesses, detaining and interrogating suspects. If required, it would carry out house-to-house searches. Sometimes suspects would be passed from *ronda* group to *ronda* group, or even from community to community, each interrogating in turn, looking for contradictions.

Whenever possible, the *ronda* leadership would try to mediate among disputing parties. If that failed, the *ronda* would bring the case before an assembly. The *comité* would present the facts as it had determined them, all parties to the dispute would be given a chance to speak, and the community as a whole would decide whether suspects were guilty and how they should be punished.

Sanctions were generally relatively mild. They usually included three elements: a public, signed act of contrition including a promise not to err anew; a punishment, such as additional nights of patrolling and days working for the community, and frequently a light beating; and some form of compensation to the aggrieved parties and the community. *Ronderos* argue that the purpose was not to so much to punish the culprits as to encourage them to change their behaviour and reintegrate them into the community. A litany many repeat with pride tells of former thieves who are now valued *ronderos.*

The following personal account gives some sense of *rondero* justice:

> *Thirteen hats were stolen from Paulino Espinoza's house, right in the town center. He notified the sector delegate. At first there were no clues, no suspects. The case was paralyzed. But about a week later there was another problem, rumors of a married woman who had been having an affair they had been seen by a certain Paco. Anyway, the senora accused Paco of spreading malicious gossip. So the* ronda *captured Paco, and Paco told her to her face that he had seen her with a man. She denied it, and nobody knew if it was true. But it was necessary to punish Paco for spreading stories, and besides which, we all knew that he was a petty thief, though we had never had proof. In other words, the senora's accusation was a useful pretext. So the* ronda *took him aside and began to whip him to get him to confess what he had robbed, and he began to talk. He admitted that he had stolen the hats, but he said that he had done it at the request of "El Chino." El Chino's real name was Wilmer. He was the son of Eliseo Carajulca, the witch, and a very dangerous man.*

The case now went to the *ronda* committee. The directors asked to read Paco's signed statement; they ordered that El Chino be detained. He was captured and taken that night to be interrogated. Everyone came. We were all afraid of Wilmer; once he hated you he always looked for a way to get even. Wilmer and Paco were put face to face. Paco told him, "You made me steal." Wilmer denied it. The ronderos whipped the suspects; still El Chino denied everything, but Paco insisted he had told the truth. And we reached the conclusion that they were guilty.

The problem was how to punish them. The ronderos tied up El Chino; they took him some 200 meters up the trail, to where the river forms a kind of lagoon. They took both of them, whipping them, and threw them in the water. Twenty minutes. Always telling them to change their ways. Paco said he was sorry, but El Chino was too macho. After that they were brought back to the assembly; the secretary read the record of everything they had said, that Paco had begged forgiveness but that El Chino had been stubborn, and they were ordered to return the hats or to pay for them. Then they were given a punishment: one night of patrols and a day of communal labour. After that Paco became a good rondero. But El Chino was always a problem.

By the mid-1980s the *rondas* were resolving vast numbers of conflicts. The Federación Provincial de Rondas Campesinas de Cajamarca reported that between 1987 and 1989 its member *rondas* had adjudicated over 12,000 disputes: 600 cases of rustling; 500 other robberies; 280 family disputes; 2,900 cases of inappropriate public behaviour; 3,500 land and water problems; 400 disputes over trails; 1,600 complaints concerning the non fulfilment of contracts; and 400 cases of witchcraft. Even if taken with a significant grain of salt, the numbers are enormous.

But, was it justice? What kind of normative framework Peruvian law/communal values underlay its administration? Was it simply arbitrary vigilantism? The vast majority of the peasants with whom I have spoken refer to peasant justice with great pride, insisting that it is impartial, fair, and compassionate. Mistakes may have been made, perhaps inevitably, but they insist these were few. Moreover, they maintain, peasant justice must be evaluated in relation to the official court system, in comparison with which it is quicker, cheaper, far more effective, and probably more just. For most of the peasants, not only was it real justice but it was the only justice available.

Yet clearly it was not a "legal" process. The Peruvian constitution expressly forbids the private administration of justice, although some reference is made to the right of communities to practice their "customary law." Nor did it follow any codified "legal" norms. Communities made decisions on the basis of their sense of what is right rather than any explicit official laws. Judgments were often based on reputation and past behaviour rather than evidence of a particular crime. Like any system of justice by popular opinion, it could be manipulated and abused.

Legal purists are often horrified by justice by popular assembly, fearing its arbitrariness and partiality. Indeed, many of the local judges and prosecutors I have interviewed have recounted lengthy lists of *ronda* abuses, both real and imagined. Defenders of peasant justice, in contrast, insist that it is based on well-understood, albeit implicit, communal norms, so-called customary law (just as they also recount an even more lengthy list of abuses, both real and imagined, by the police and official courts). However, there is a more subtle interpretation.

It has an essentially dynamic character, but that does not imply any extreme arbitrary use or the capricious creation of momentary norms. What is the justice pursued? In the first place, it is mediation of interests, putting an end to conflicts that have broken the peace of the community. The objective is not to isolate or eliminate the individual, but to reintegrate him into the social life of the group. Sanctions are determined according to the conditions and ability of the person to fulfil the punishment. The purpose of sanctions is not restitution to the aggrieved party, but rather the good of the community as a whole. Reincidence is punished severely. The more a problem has repercussions on communal life, the more serious is the sanction.

Ronderos themselves make similar points:

> *When there is a problem between ronderos, first we air everything in an assembly, then we make them embrace, they eat from the same plate, and they ask forgiveness of each other.*

What is important, is that the punishment is a public one. It has a moral force. And that is why in general people correct their behaviour. That's not the way it is with official justice. There they put you in a cell, where no one can see you, they accept money, and then they let you go.

Only if we understand peasant justice in these terms can we grasp the *rondas'* use of force. In reviewing a number of cases, the overall mildness of sanctions was impressive.

Seldom were the peasants punished severely, even those accused of serious theft. Sanctions, which were always public, usually involved no more than a few nights of patrols, a few days of communal labour and perhaps but not always a light beating. It often seemed that the guiding principle was less some abstract concept of justice than accommodation, finding an agreement with which all could live. Just as the accused were asked to confess in public, their accusers were asked to forgive. Incarceration, which would drag out conflicts and hurt families, was never used. Great care was taken to avoid giving rise to feuds.

However, on occasion sanctions could be severe. For example, I was told of a case in early 1995 of a professional rustler, the head of a complex network, who had been sanctioned previously a number of times. He was brought before an assembly of sixteen communities that decided that he be beaten two times by each community a total of thirty-two whippings and then be given a month of nightly patrols accompanied by daily communal labour, a punishment of considerable physical severity. His case, however, was an exception, for in continuing to steal he had defied the authority of the *ronda.* What was being punished was not the crime but the defiance.

Interrogations in particular often involve the use of force, though severe force is uncommon and death most unusual. However, whippings, dunkings in lagoons, long marches (sometimes barefoot), physical exercise, and public humiliation are all used to extract information.

Administering justice in these terms may be, as the peasants claim, fairer, quicker, more efficient, and perhaps even more just than the formal Peruvian justice system, but it is not without costs. It brings the *rondas* into a permanent tension with the judiciary, rooted in legal issues, corruption, professional jealousy, and the peasants' use of force. Peruvian law gives the *rondas* no clear legal right to administer justice. In doing so the *rondas* are usurping functions reserved to the judicial power. In detaining suspects they are guilty of crimes against individual liberty; and in using physical force during interrogation they are guilty of assault. Those whom the *rondas* would punish are quick to take advantage of the *rondas'* situation, and there have been dozens if not hundreds of cases in which peasants sanctioned by the *rondas* have denounced them to the authorities. In Bambamarca, for example, the provincial federation, the Central Unica de Rondas Campesinas, estimated that between 1990 and 1995 more than 140 ronderos had faced charges. For those so accused, cases can drag on for years and the cost in lawyers' fees, travel, and perhaps bribes can be enormous.

The following case, though exceptional in its complexity, gives a sense of the problem. In October 1992, an elderly woman from the hamlet of Huangamarca was riding in a dense fog across a mountain pass in the neighbouring village of Huilcate. Suddenly she lost control of her mule, and it plunged into the underbrush and reared. In her panic she thought she saw a cadaver. Upon arriving at Huangamarca, she informed the *ronda,* which requested permission to investigate from the *ronda* of Huilcate. The two *rondas* searched the pass but found nothing.

The case, however, did not end there. Someone informed the police in the provincial capital of Bambamarca. A week later, the police sent notification to the *rondas* in strong language demanding the *rondas* investigate further, implying that they were covering up a crime. The *rondas* again organized an investigation. This time they detained a suspect, Francisco Díaz. There was nothing specific linking him to the crime (it was not even clear that a crime had occurred), but the police were insisting in threatening tones that the *rondas* do something, and Díaz was thoroughly disliked, known in the communities as a bully and troublemaker. Five years before he had been implicated in another murder, but he had fled the area for a time and was never punished.

Díaz was detained for less than a week, but during that

time he was brought before two assemblies, each with as many as 800 peasants in attendance, and taken from sector to sector and interrogated, finally confessing. He later alleged to the police (probably with police encouragement) that he had been brutally tortured, beaten and kicked in the groin and head, and threatened with execution by ten masked *ronderos* whom he could not identify. The *rondas* deny they used physical force.

By now, however, Díaz's family had notified the police. who came to rescue the prisoner and arrest the *ronderos.* Charges of usurpation, assault, and kidnapping were brought against twenty-eight peasants. Their cases, appealed to the departmental court, dragged on for more than 2 years. In the end for some the charges were dropped, and others received suspended sentences.

The *ronderos* see in cases like these monumental hypocrisy: criminals go free, while they are accused, charged, and even imprisoned for administering justice. Few peasants believe they have broken the law, at least any reasonable law. They do not perceive detaining a suspect as kidnapping. If they use a bit of force, so do the police. Virtually all see the above as major problems facing their organization.

Indeed, by the early 1990s, many peasants felt that the *rondas* had entered into a crisis. A number of factors had come together to weaken the organization, but in the peasants' eyes by far the most important were the repeated accusations. As a result, a discussion broke out within the *rondas,* at both the level of the federations and at the grass roots, over how to respond. Central to the discussion was a debate over peasant justice and the propriety of violence.

Human Rights and the *Rondas*

Before the 1980s human rights did not figure prominently in Peruvian political discourse. Historically, the political opposition had focused more on economic needs than political rights, formulating demands in a rhetoric that emphasized class (and even "armed") struggle rather than democracy. Beginning in the 1970s, however, two developments placed human rights on the political agenda.

The first was the emergence of a progressive movement within the Catholic Church. In his book, *The Theology of Liberation,* Gustavo Gutierrez called on the church to commit itself to accompanying the poor, those "non persons" whose humanity is barely acknowledged, in their struggles for change. In hundreds of parishes across rural Peru, priests and sisters began efforts to reach out to the peasantry, training lay catechists, organizing Bible reflection groups, and preaching a theology of human dignity and grassroots empowerment. In doing so they began to engage the poor in a dialogue over dignity and rights.

The other factor was the explosion of political violence that erupted in the 1980s the Shining Path and the Tupac Amaru Revolutionary Movement uprisings, and the brutal, indiscriminate state response. Caught between guerrilla accusations that they were lackeys of capitalism and the state's suspicion they were front groups for subversion, significant segments of the Marxist left began to re-evaluate the importance, and assume the discourse, of human rights. A second result of subversion and the state's "dirty war" was the emergence of a vibrant human rights network, one that actively denounced both guerrilla and state abuses and struggled to place human rights on the Peruvian political agenda. For many at the grass roots who were besieged by the violence the new human rights organizations became important allies. Thus by the late 1980s the idea of "human rights" was part of the political ambience, even in those regions like the *ronda* provinces of Cajamarca where neither guerrilla nor state violence were major problems.

It was in this atmosphere that the discussion in the *rondas* over peasant justice took place. External actors played significant roles. The Marxist left was perhaps the least important, even though two parties in particular, Patria Roja and PUM, had developed close ties to the *rondas* since the very beginning. Both parties had contributed to the early organization of the patrols, and through the years had provided advice, political protection, and support; indeed, many *ronderos* were militants on the left. But by the late 1980s the left was mired in its own crisis, caught in its struggle with the Shining Path for political space, encumbered by its traditional language of confrontation, and suffering a crisis of identity following the collapse of Soviet communism. While still a valuable ally to the peasants, the left was unable to articulate an unambiguous position on rights.

The progressive faction in the Catholic Church played a far more significant role. Many of the actively religious felt a deep commitment to the *rondas* that was rooted in a theology of human dignity, empowerment, and "accompaniment." Priests, sisters, and bishops worked hard, albeit not always publicly, to support the *ronda* organization, providing counsel, protection, and resources. Lay catechists had figured prominently among the original *ronda* founders and later leaders. Yet many of these pastoral workers were from early on quietly critical of what they saw as the *rondas'* excesses, and they worked actively to communicate that message to the peasants. In repeated seminars and weekly encounters, catechists were encouraged to reflect on the idea of human rights, understood as human dignity and responsibility, and to encourage Christian and *ronda* groups in their communities to do the same. The church also organized courses for *ronda* leaders. In Chota, the bishop began in the early 1990s to convene annual retreats of *ronda* leaders and catechists to discuss problems the organization faced. A repeated theme was that of violence and the accusations.

The following, from a catechist who became a *ronda* leader, captures the importance of the church's activity.

The language of human rights entered around 1988, through the influence of the church and the catechists. I have been to three courses, one in Chota for catechists, another in Cajamarca for ronderos and state officials, and then another in Chota for catechists. In them I learned what human rights are and why they are important. I studied the constitution and the rights that it guarantees, the right to life, the right not to be mistreated, the right not to be held incommunicado, the rights of children, etc. From those courses I carried the message of rights to the bases, in assemblies, and in conversations, when we reached agreements solving disputes. At first the people wouldn't listen because there was a contradiction with what they did, but gradually we have won them over, in part because they saw that violating rights has brought them problems, in part because they have begun to understand.

By the late 1980s national human rights groups were also becoming influential. They too felt a deep commitment to the *rondas,* one rooted in a belief in "peasant rights" and citizenship. Like the church, they offered advice, education, protection, and, in particular, legal counsel. However, in two ways their message was subtly different from that of the church. First, it was rooted more explicitly in international human rights norms, not simply in grassroots empowerment. Second, the human rights groups were more aware of the tension between local autonomy and individual rights, hence they were more interested in finding ways to mesh the two. The human rights groups went beyond simply offering a general education on rights in pamphlets, seminars, and radio programs. They also organized retreats that brought together judges and prosecutors with ronderos to discuss peasant and state justice, they sponsored courses to train justices of the peace, and they offered counsel on how to investigate without using violence.

At first the idea didn't catch on at the grass roots, but it did in the federation, and we tried to push it, so that the ronderos would know the laws. In Huangamarca we organized four courses, and in all the other hamlets. To make the *rondas* understand that they should not commit errors.

It was in this atmosphere in which economic crisis and political violence had placed human rights on the national agenda, in which the peasants felt that their organization was in crisis (in part because of the repeated legal accusations), and in which the church, national human rights groups, and, less clearly, the left were trying to protect the organization and at the same time influence its behavior that the discussion on peasant justice took place. It was never a formal discussion, a debate that reached a clear conclusion, but rather an ever present theme whenever *ronderos* gathered to discuss their problems.

The discussion has centered on basically four positions, pulling in opposite directions. On the one hand, (1) the peasants feel that if the *rondas* do not exercise force in administering justice, they will be unable to establish respect and impose *ronda* authority. Peasant justice is, after all, informal justice. It is not backed by the authority and power of the state; the *rondas* have no legal right to adjudicate disputes; and they have no legal right to demand compliance. Why should rustlers respect them? Why should those who might fear the decisions of communal assemblies not appeal to the courts or the police instead? (2) Justice demands interrogation, and, in the perception of many of the peasants, successful interrogation demands intimidation. How else can they make the criminals confess? After all, the police use force to extract confessions, and they are never punished. Why should the *rondas* be punished for doing what the police do? On the other hand, (3) the constant accusations have weakened the *rondas,* and their use of force exposes the *rondas* to criminal charges. The cost of peasant justice, for the *rondas* and their leaders, is too high. And (4) the core of the *rondas'* claim to legitimacy is that they stand for justice, and justice involves respect for human rights. How can the peasants justify doing precisely what they criticize the state for doing?

The discussion has not been conclusive; no consensus has been achieved. In each community there are some who, either from fear of legal sanctions or conviction, argue for restraint, just as there are others who see the authority of the *rondas* at stake.

In the assemblies one finds a bit of everything. There is always someone who gets excited and yells, "Let's really give it to him hard." But there are always others who are more moderate, young people who say there should be other ways. Sometimes the hotheads sway the people. Sometimes we catechists have to enter the debate to calm things down.

Some peasants express a clear commitment:

> *Our community has always been more moderate. Personally I've never participated in a dunking; maybe that's because I did not like to see such things.*

Others are more ambivalent:

> *We hardly use any force anymore. Now we know about human rights. But the problem is that if we don't use force, the crooks won't tell us what they know.*

The provincial federation of Bambamarca, the Central, has tried to straddle the fence:

> *We have recommended from the Central that the* rondas *shouldn't give more than ten lashes at the most. That was an agreement reached in a provincial assembly. Ten don't hurt that much; its not like before. And the doctor won't say it's much either. Of course, it varies with the crime. And we tell the bases that they should always consider other sanctions too.*

When asked, almost everyone today denies that force is being used: "perhaps elsewhere but certainly not in our hamlet." However, when pressed, most admit that an occasional whipping still occurs, although they insist, probably truthfully, much less than in earlier years.

This is so at least in part because the *rondas* have become more skilled at investigation. Through advice and training from human rights lawyers and through their own experience, they have learned that coercion is not the only way to obtain information and they have developed increasingly sophisticated techniques.

The *rondas* still investigate, but they use far less physical force. For example, now we will take into account antecedents. Then we will find out what the suspect was doing at the time of the problem. Then we will see if there are other witnesses. And then we will question. Most people will talk; they are afraid. But some are pretty sly and won't. Then we have different groups question them to see if they make mistakes. We will look for inconsistencies. Last we apply pressure threatening force. Usually that is more than enough. If the crime is really serious and the suspect resists, we may use a little force, a few lashes, but not many anymore.

Now we don't have that image of strength. When I was younger I really liked punishing. But I've learned that it brings us problems. (But can't you administer justice, earn respect, without punishing?) Yes, but less. That's why the people don't believe in it quite as much as they used to.

The discussion continues.

Summary

It is my belief that, increasingly, it does. That is not because a commitment to individual rights is part of the cultural tradition of rural communities. Peasants have always spoken of their oppression and in their struggles have referred to "rights," but such rights were conceived more in communal than individual terms. But, as the *rondas* have tried to carve out a space for relative communal autonomy, as they have tried to administer justice where the state has failed, and as in that process they have encountered enemies as well as allies in a nation wracked by economic crisis and political violence, not only have they become acquainted with the idea of individual rights, but the idea has also acquired meaning to them.

5

Perspectives of Western Human Rights Theories

Introduction

The theorists whose concepts of rights are described here Emmanuel Mounier, Jacques Maritain, and Roberto Unger have each independently elaborated a conception of rights based on Western philosophy and social thought which differs radically from traditional liberal conceptions by, *inter alia*, its inclusion of economic and social rights (and, in the case of Mounier and Maritain, of group rights) in the catalogue of human rights. Emmanuel Mounier was the editor of the intellectual French journal *Esprit* during the 1930s and 1940s and the leading member of a movement known as "Personalism" in France. He died in 1950. Jacques Maritain was a French philosopher well known in Europe, Latin America, and North America. Serving on the faculty at Princeton for a number of years, he lectured widely at American and Canadian universities during the 1940s and 1950s; he died in 1973. Roberto Unger, a Brazilian social theorist and leading figure in the Critical Legal Studies movement, is presently teaching at Harvard Law School.

Although a number of philosophers and social theorists of the nineteenth and twentieth centuries could be considered as adopting personalist or communitarian perspectives, I have chosen to limit this essay to the contributions of Mounier, Maritain, and Unger because they have explicitly formulated detailed catalogues of rights. All three have been critical of the individualist and property-oriented approach of Western liberalism, while also rejecting Marxist collectivism. Each views his conception of rights not as a gloss on liberal or Marxist approaches but as a distinct theoretical approach. I have used the phrase "personalist perspectives" or "personalist-communitarian perspectives" to express the common aspects of their individual approaches to rights. The philosophical and social theories of these three men are certainly not identical, but in their approach to rights there is a striking similarity. The concept of the "person" or "personality" is an essential element of their social and political theory: they distinguish the concept of "person" from the concept of the "individual" by an emphasis on the intrinsic links between persons and community.

A number of contemporary scholars have criticized the limitations of the liberal conception of rights, but few have made constructive contributions to a revised theory of rights. Mounier, Maritain, and Unger have attempted to do so. Personalist perspectives on rights are rarely discussed in contemporary literature on the theory of human rights. This essay is an endeavour to bring this alternative approach into public debate, not only the academic and intellectual debate, but the cross-cultural and political debate, since the personalist approach like the liberal or Marxist has implications for political choices.

Liberal ideology, based on eighteenth-century Enlightenment philosophy, emphasizes the freedom of individuals, civil and political rights, contractually based obligations and, in particular, property rights. Liberal ideology encompasses with difficulty, if at all, economic, social, and group rights. Marxist ideology has been critical of liberal conceptions of rights, considering them to be "bourgeois rights" which sustain power relations in society. Marxists have emphasized economic and social rights. These two ideological approaches have occupied center stage in discussions of human rights in the West. Neither approach is fully in harmony with the perspective on rights contained in the International Bill of Human Rights. Ideological disputes among proponents of the two approaches have also been detrimental to the development of human rights theory and practice.

The problematic of Western philosophical thought on human rights is whether it is possible within the Western cultural tradition to conceptualize a theory of rights which retains the important concept of individual rights, but also regards some rights as inhering in groups and some rights as entailing positive entitlements to a basic level of economic sufficiency. The inclusion of economic and social rights and group rights in the catalogue of human rights has been forcefully criticized by many in the West as lacking logical and philosophical coherence. Maurice Cranston, an ardent defender of the individualist conception of rights, has expressed this objection most forcefully. He argues for a "philosophically respectable concept of human rights" not "muddied, obscured and debilitated by an attempt to incorporate rights of a different logical category" such as economic, social, and group rights. Personalist perspectives on rights, which are becoming increasingly common in the West, demonstrate that a philosophically sound theory of rights may be based on Western cultural traditions and yet not be hidebound by a constrained liberal tradition of rights. Personalist-communitarian perspectives that emphasize that the person lives in community with others and not as an isolated individual represent an evolution within Western culture and provide a more coherent contemporary approach to rights than eighteenth-century liberalism or nineteenth-century Marxism.

This seemingly theoretical controversy over "rights" has practical consequences. The perception of rights adopted in a particular culture reflects and influences aspects of social life. Abdullahi A. An-Na'im points out elsewhere in this collection that the inadequacy or lack of cultural legitimacy of human rights standards is one of the main underlying causes of violation of those standards. Advocates for the homeless and for adequate health care for all in North America have grasped the practical importance of the conceptualization of rights and refer to the "right to housing" and a "right to health care." An-Na'im argues persuasively that internal discourse within particular cultural traditions including the Western is a necessary element in developing cross-cultural legitimacy for human rights standards. He invites those of us who are human rights scholars and activists to examine our own cultural tradition, to recognize not only its values but also its limitations and obstacles to a full perception of human dignity. The Western liberal tradition of rights has made substantial contributions to the concept of civil and political rights. But one of its limitations is the inadequate recognition of what economic inequality and deprivation signify for human dignity.

Western rights theory has been criticized by non-Westerners more fully conscious of the glaring disparity between wealth and poverty in the world. Non-Westerners have also criticized the excessive individualist orientation of Western rights theory, since "community" and the role of groups are perceived as particularly important within many non-Western cultures. In many parts of the world, the most egregious violations of human dignity are the degrading poverty and inhumane conditions of life of millions of individuals, giving rise to a growing conviction that any conception of human rights must encompass economic and social rights. Upendra Baxi, an Indian academic and activist, has expressed this perception well, paraphrasing Ronald Dworkin's work, *Taking Rights Seriously*, by referring to the need to "take suffering seriously."

The preoccupations evident in Mounier, Maritain, and Unger's theories of rights grow out of contemporary historical experiences and resemble the preoccupations expressed by many non-Western commentators on rights. All three view human rights standards as evolving over time and as reflecting particular historical circumstances. Thus, new standards may evolve depending on newly perceived social needs; also, evolution is possible within particular cultural traditions These basic perceptions indicate an openness to evolution within the Western cultural tradition, an openness that seems requisite to appreciating the approaches of other cultural traditions.

Personalist Perspectives of Mounier, Maritain and unger

The terms "personalism" and "personalist" have been used in a number of philosophical, theological, and political contexts in the twentieth century. An emphasis on the concept of personality can be traced far back in Western philosophical and theological thought, however. Although many differences are apparent among thinkers using these terms, a common thread appears to be conceptualizing the "person" as essentially part of a community, thus distinguishing the "person" from the "individual" regarded as an isolated entity. *The Encylopedia of Philosophy* defines personalism as A philosophical perspective or system for which person is the ontological ultimate and for which personality is thus the fundamental explanatory principle. Explicitly developed in the twentieth century, personalism in its historical antecedents and its dominant themes has close affiliations with and affinities to other systems that are not strictly personalist.

In using the plural term "perspectives," I emphasize that there is no single personal perspective but rather that a personalist approach is evident in the social theory of a number of scholars and activists whose thinking is not identical in all respects. It would be impossible in the space available here to do justice to the many movements and theorists who have identified themselves as personalists or have used the terms "personality" or "personalism" extensively in their writings. *The Encylopedia of Philosophy* refers to two major personalist philosophies: first, American personalism, which it calls "idealistic personalism," and second, "realistic personalism," which is primarily European. *The Encylopedia* states that "personalism has been decisively influenced by both the Greek metaphysical and Biblical religious motifs of the dominant Western theological tradition." American personalism is closely linked to the schools of philosophy and Protestant theology at Boston University, where it had been a major influence since the early nineteenth century.

Mounier, Maritain, and Unger appear to be representative of realist personalism. All three use the terms "personality," personalism," and "community" frequently; and I consider that they share a personalist perspective, although their perspectives differ in a number of respects. Sufficient commonalities exist to justify treating them as sharing a common perspective.

Emmanuel Mounier was born in France in 1905 and died in 1950. A philosopher by education, he was best known as the editor of the intellectual French journal *Esprit* and the proponent of a movement called *personalism.* Mounier's personalist movement is little known in the AngloAmerican world but is well known in France and certain circles in Latin America. Mounier was a left-wing Catholic who disliked Christian Democracy. He has been called "a serious Christian who wanted to be a social revolutionary." Mounier had an openness to secular social movements unusual in French Catholicism in the early part of the twentieth century. Although he revolted against the bourgeois conservative Catholicism prevalent in his youth, he remained a convinced Christian throughout his life and early became committed to balancing deep religiosity and concern for social justice. To Mounier, Christianity was the most radical of countercultures, yet he found Marxists and atheists exhibiting more charity than Christians in France. By the time of Mounier's death, French Catholicism had become more known for its commitment to social justice through worker-priests and other movements than for its traditional bourgeois conservatism. Mounier and the personalist movement contributed to this extraordinary change in French Catholicism. While embracing a humane socialism, Mounier was not a Marxist, however. He accepted neither the concept of class struggle nor historical determinism.

Jacques Maritain was a French natural law philosopher active in crosscultural discussions on rights under UNESCO auspices at the time of the drafting of the Universal Declaration of Human Rights. His formulation of rights is outlined in *The Rights of Man and Natural Law*, published in 1944, and in *Man and the State*, published in 1959. Well known in the United States and Canada through his books and for his teaching and lecturing at Princeton University and at the Universities of Chicago and Toronto, he died in 1973 at the age of 91. His extensive philosophical and social writings are influential in natural law circles in Europe and North and South America. Maritain used the terms "political humanism" and "personalism" to refer to his approach to rights theory. He had been involved with Mounier in the initial phases of the development of the journal *Esprit* but at a later period distanced himself from the Mounier personalist movement. Maritain maintained that it is possible for persons holding widely differing beliefs on the justification for human rights to agree on a body of practical human rights standards.

Roberto Unger is a social theorist who divides his time between his appointment on the faculty of Harvard Law School and political participation in his native Brazil. He is primarily identified with the Critical Legal Studies movement in North America. Although Unger does not refer to himself as a "personalist," nor does he refer in his writings to the influence of European or American personalists, I consider him as expressing a personalist-communitarian perspective because of his emphasis on personality and community as essential aspects of his social theory. His formulation of rights theory, like those of Mounier and Maritain, is neither Marxist nor liberal. In elaborating a visionary program of "empowered democracy" he advocates a "personalist program" and a transformed conception of "community" supported by a theory of rights.

The perspectives of these three thinkers are characterized by certain similarities cited here. Focusing only on their commonalities perhaps does an injustice to the development of the individual social and political theories of these three scholars, each of whom has written extensively. Maritain published more than seventy books during his long life. Mounier developed his concept of personalism over many years in the issues of the journal *Esprit*. Unger has thus far published five major volumes on social theory. Mounier's conception of a "personalist and communitarian revolution," Maritain's elaboration of "political humanism," and Unger's visionary program of "empowered democracy" each warrant far more individual consideration than can be given here. The emphasis in this chapter is, however, necessarily on their commonalities rather than their differences. Each of their social theories shares the following perspectives, which have, in turn, influenced their conceptions of rights:

1. an emphasis on the concept of the "person" as distinguished from the concept of the "individual";
2. the view that the term "person" implies relationships with others in a community and a corresponding emphasis on community and the relations between persons and society;
3. a focus on the roles and rights not only of individuals but also of communities, particularly communities smaller than the state: families, groups linked by common cultural ties, local communities, consumer

or occupational groups, and so on, and a corresponding view that rights may be claimed against groups as well as against states;

4. the effort to distinguish their social theories from both Marxist collectivism and liberal capitalism;
5. an emphasis on *praxis*, or the practical implications of their social theories.

Person and Community

The definition of personalism quoted earlier from *The Encyclopedia of Philosophy* fails to mention an aspect of personalism considered essential by most of those using the term, namely, the communitarian or social implications of the concept of "personality." Max Scheler, a German phenomenologist, philosopher, and personalist who influenced Mounier, considered that "the person as all individual emerges only within a circle of other persons in sociality the person is inseparable from the context of the world and others." Mounier's "first expositions of personalism were notable in their new concern for community, a need to form 'collective persons' and 'persons of persons'." Mounier consistently referred to his movement as "a personalist and *communitarian* revolution." In his view, the "true community was a reality as fundamental as that of the person."

In a fine study on personalism which includes extensive information on the roots of the personalism of a number of European thinkers, Jean Lacroix has written:

> *To be a person is to transform the "one" into the "we." The person always lives in a world peopled by other persons the notion of person always entails an elan which carries one beyond one's self.*

Lacroix considers personalism not as constituting a philosophy but as providing an inspiration for various philosophies. While emphasizing the concept of the person, he points out that the individualist and the personalist approaches should not be seen as radically opposed but as complementary. Both aspects are important.

Maritain has written that his conception of society is *personalist*. . . and *communal*, because it recognizes the fact that the person tends naturally towards society and communion, in particular towards the political community, and because, in the specifically political sphere and to the extent that man is a part of political society, it considers the common good superior to that of individuals.

Unger states that his whole program of "empowered democracy" can "be read as a vision of the forms and conditions of human community." In emphasizing the importance of personal relationship to the development of the institutions of an empowered democracy he writes that "at the center of this revised approach to direct personal relations stands a conception of community as a zone in which the increased acceptance of mutual vulnerability makes it possible to multiply ways of diminishing the conflict between attachment to other people and the claims of self-consciousness and self-possession."

Intermediate Organizations or Groups

All three thinkers have emphasized the significance of communities smaller than the state. Maritain speaks of the important role of "autonomous agencies" within the polity and emphasizes "associative forms of industrial ownership" by workers as an example of the role which such agencies should play in economic life. He writes that his conception of a society of free men is *pluralist*, because it assumes that the development of the human person normally requires a plurality of autonomous communities which have their own rights, liberties and authority; among these communities there are some of a rank inferior to the political state, which arise either from the fundamental exigencies of nature (as in the case of the family community) or else from the will of persons freely coming together to form diverse groups. Other communities are of a rank superior to the State, as in the temporal realm, that organized international Community towards which we aspire today.

Mounier not only propounded a theory of community but also became the leader of the personalist movement in France that grouped together a small community of like-minded persons linked in one manner or another to the journal *Esprit*. Unger writes of the role of grassroots organizations and the need for decentralization in economic decision making. An emphasis on intermediate groups influenced the conceptions of rights of all three thinkers.

Liberal Individualism and Marxist Collectivism

Maritain, Mounier, and Unger have explicitly distinguished their personalist vision or orientation from both liberal individualism and Communist collectivism. In describing the personalism of Mounier, John Hellman writes:

> *The assertion of the 'absolute value of the human person' was not simply an abstract affirmation of human dignity but rather a movement of defence against two antithetical threats. It mirrored the desperate effort of intellectuals in the early nineteen-thirties to navigate a 'third way' between capitalism and communism.*

Scheler viewed both Marxism and liberalism as "seeing politics in terms of self-interest and material welfare," rejecting both for a personalist vision. Maritain writes:

> *Those whom, for want of a better name, I just called the advocates of a liberal-individualist type of society; see the mark of human dignity first and foremost in the power of each person to appropriate individually the goods of nature in order to do freely whatever he wants; the advocates of a communistic type of society the mark of human dignity first and foremost in the power to submit these same goods to the collective command of the society body in order to 'free' human labour (by subduing it to the economic community) and to gain the control of history; the advocates of a personalistic type of society see the mark of human dignity first and foremost in the power to make these same goods of nature serve the common conquest of intrinsically human, moral, and spiritual goods and of man's freedom of autonomy. As far as I am concerned, I know where I stand: with the third of the three schools of thought I just mentioned.*

Unger states that the Critical Legal Studies movement, of which he is a leading member, is within the "tradition of leftist tendencies in modern legal thought." He also says, however, that his social theory is liberal, even superliberal. In fact, his social theory and his rights theories cannot be placed squarely within either traditional Marxist or traditional liberal thought.

Personalism and Praxis

As social and political theorists, Maritain, Mounier, and Unger have all been concerned with the practical implications of their theory. None has been solely concerned with speculative philosophical or social systems, although all three have based practice on theory.

The dust jacket of *Passion, An Essay on Personality* reports that Unger is an "active participant in the politics of his native Brazil [;] he has helped develop political programs and party platforms." Unger's professed aim is activist, that is, the "development of practices and institutions that prevent factions, classes or any other specially placed groups from gaining control over the key resources of a society (wealth, power, knowledge)." Although Unger finds social democracy the nearest approach to his social theory, he finds it too, constrained by entrenched social roles and hierarchies; he refers to his social theory as a "radical alternative to social democracy." But, he maintains, his theory must be translated into action: "The institutional ideas have to be realized by collective action. They remain unpersuasive and dreamlike until we have complemented them with a view of the social activities that might establish them."

Mounier organized a community of friends at Chatenay-Malabry in France, but his contribution to practical action is also demonstrated in the pages of *Esprit*, where contemporary issues in French political and social life were widely discussed, focusing particularly on issues of labour and education. John Hellman has described Mounier's community as follows:

> *A great source of consolation and hope for Mounier was the personalist community which he founded at Chatenay-Malabry. Six or seven intellectuals and their families could live comfortably in Les Murs Blancs. At first they all ate meals in common but this was soon abandoned in favour of periodic, optional, common meals. A happy balance was achieved between privacy and community life, intellectual and spiritual collaboration, and the pursuit of individual careers. For several decades, some of France's leading intellectual figures have lived in friendship and harmony at Chatenay-Malabry, living in community according to Mounier's inspiration. Self-conscious avant-garde Christians, they have welcomed visitors from around the world and sought to demonstrate by example that their personalism is more than an intellectual position.*

The community continued long after Mounier's death in 1950. Personalism, as developed by Mouner and others linked to *Esprit*, was less a philosophy than "a method for thinking and living." Practical implications were fundamental to the movement.

Jacques Maritain was a philosopher who wrote widely on subjects of political and social theory. His writings were frequently related to current political and social issues, although he took no active part in political life. In one of his best-known books, *True Humanism, A Charter of Social Action*, he expressed the practical orientation of his concerns:

> *The questions dealt with here belong to that section of philosophy which Aristotle and St. Thomas called* Practical, *since in a general way it includes the whole philosophy of human action. Practical philosophy is still philosophy and remains a mode of speculative knowledge; but, unlike metaphysics or natural philosophy, it is from the outset directed to action as its object, and however large a part verification of fact may play in it, however much it must needs take historical necessities and conditions into account, it is above all a science, of freedom.*

Maritain wrote, among other things, on the relation between religious and temporal concerns and between church and state, on the rights of workers on democracy, and on an international political order. While he did not take an active role in political affairs, he expressed himself on current political issues, protesting the bombing of Madrid and Guernica by the Franco forces at a time when many of his fellow Catholics in France and elsewhere were supporting Franco against the Loyalists, whom they regarded as persecutors of the Church. He became part of the French delegation to the second Conference of UNESCO held in Mexico City and participated actively in early discussions aimed at elaborating a truly international conception of human rights. Particularly in his later books, Maritain evidenced a continuing concern for the political and social implications of his philosophical orientation.

Personalism and Human Rights

Of particular interest for this essay is the detailed formulation of rights elaborated by Mounier, Maritain, and Unger. Emmanuel Mounier drafted a declaration of rights together with other members of the French personalist movement between 1941 and 1944; Maritain described his conception of rights in *The Rights of Man and Natural Law* published in 1944, and in *Man and the State*, published in 1951; Unger has developed an original conceptualization of rights in his latest book, *False Necessity*, published in 1987. Although these elaborations of rights are not identical, they share a number of elements. Each of them includes economic and social rights, as well as individual rights, in his categorization of rights; all of them maintain that individual rights can be claimed as a protection against group tyranny as well as against state action.

Reformulation of the French Declaration of Rights

During the Nazi occupation of France, a group of personalists led by Mounier drafted clandestinely a declaration of rights which they believed corrected the rationalism and individualism of the 1789 French Declaration of the Rights of Man and Citizen and which they intended would serve as a model for a treaty to be signed by like-minded states after World War II. This innovative catalogue of rights was one of the mode declarations of rights that influenced the drafters of the revised French Declaration of Rights adopted in 1946. In 1989, the two-hundredth anniversary, of the drafting of the French Declaration of the Rights of Man and Citizen, We heard much about that 1789 Declaration. We heard little, however, of the revision of the French Declaration that was adopted as the Preamble to the 1946 French Constitution, which established the Fourth Republic. The 1789 Declaration is reprinted in most collections of human rights instruments; the revised formulation is not. The historical importance of the 1789 Declaration is evident, but the state where it originated has determined that it no longer adequately reflects its contemporary conception of rights. Jean Rivero has pointed out that In the intervening two centuries between the time the Declaration of the Rights of Man and Citizen was passed in 1789 and now, the Declaration's original conception, both as an ideology and its translation into law, have undergone so many modifications that what prevails today only partially reflects the original document.

The rights recognized in the 1789 Declaration were limited to liberty, property, security, and resistance to oppression. The 1946 Declaration, in contrast, incorporates a recognition of economic and social rights. The intellectual background to the inclusion of these rights in the 1946 French Constitution and the philosophical and social reflections of French thinkers that led to the revision of the 1789 Declaration are of interest in the context of personalism. Certainly, Marxist influence played a part in the revision of the Declaration; other influences were also important, however, including the influence of the declaration of rights prepared by Mounier. The personalist declaration influenced particularly the Mouvement Republicain Populaire (MRP), the Christian Democratic party, and one of the three major political parties that participated in the drafting of the declaration eventually included in the 1946 French Constitution. Their support of the personalist declaration was ironic in view of Mounier's well-known dislike of Christian democratic parties.The initial draft ot the personalist declaration was presented for debate in the pages of *Esprit* in 1944. In a subsequent issues a number of perceptive comments were made on the draft by jurists, professors, international lawyers, and other members of the personalist movement. In 1945, the final draft of the declaration appeared in Esprit. Entitled *"Declaration of the Rights of Persons and Communities,"* it began:

> *The undersigned States recognize the authority over individuals and societies of a certain number of rights attaching to the existence of the human community, not deriving either from the individual or the state, but having double roots:*
>
> *1. The good of persons*
>
> *2. The life and normal development of persons within the natural communities where they, have been placed: families, nations, geographic and munities groups, work communities, affinity groups and groups based on particular beliefs.*

The proper function of the State is to actively assist both the independence of persons and the life of communities: the first, against the menacing tyranny of groups; the second, against the constantly reborn anarchy of individuals. An organism independent of the State should be established to judge the abuses of power by the State.

Part 1 of the declaration relates to the "Rights of Persons." In twenty six articles it lists most of the traditional civil and political rights, including also under that heading rights to health, to work, to the minimum resources necessary for "a life worthy of man," to necessary leisure, and to social security. Each of the rights is spelled out in some detail. Civil and political rights and economic and social rights are not divided into separate categories.

Part 2 of the personalist declaration is labeled, "Rights

of Communities." One of the most divisive Issues in contemporary human rights theory and practice is whether groups have rights as well as individuals. The issue has great practical importance for indigenous peoples and ethnic groups. Perceiving the existential need for a concept of group rights, a number of theorists are endeavoring to fit a concept of group rights into liberal ideology. Michael McDonald, for instance, has discussed the difficulty of doing so. Group rights can be made to fit the liberal ideology, which is fundamentally individualistic, only by stretching the concept of liberalism until it snaps and is no longer recognizable as liberalism. A different ideology is required. A concept of group rights is an essential aspect of Mounier's personalist perspective. The personalist declaration also recognizes individual rights and, as is apparent from the excerpt quoted above, the personalist regards rights as a protection against the "tyranny of groups" as well as against the tyranny of the state. In the 1940s in France, the concept of rights for groups was supported not only by personalist. The conviction of the importance of collectivities intermediate between the individual and the state had been "in the air" in Europe for a long time.

Article 27 expresses the basic approach of the section of the declaration on the rights of communities:

> *There exist natural communities. Born outside the State, they cannot be subject to it. Their spontaneous powers limit the power of the State. They should be represented as such within the State.*

Twelve articles are included under the heading of rights of communities; they relate to the rights of families, the nation, economic and work communities, and the international community. These articles join in a single statement of rights a number of concerns of contemporary international life, concerns that have seldom been joined, even after forty-five years, in a single declaration of rights, either nationally or internationally.

Article 29 relates to self determination:

> *Each nation possesses a absolute right to the independence of its culture, its language, its spiritual life, but not to unconditional political sovereignty.*
>
> *Each nation must protect, within the limits of its cohesiveness, its regional communities and ethnic, linguistic or religious groups.*

The rejection of both an unconditional free-enterprise system and a Marxist system of production is expressed in Article 30:

> *Economic communities and occupational communities are based on the service rendered and not on acquired privileges or the power of money. They should not serve essentially the profit, production or power of the State, but the needs of free consumption in conditions respecting the dignity of the worker and the development of the spirit of enterprise.*

Article 33 relates to the use of economic resources and presages the later development of concepts of "the common heritage of mankind" and the "new international economic order":

> *The human community is the beneficial owner of the totality of the riches of the universe. Each nation has the right, within the general organization, to receive its just share. Each worker has the right to emigrate, to the limit of possibilities, so that his subsistence might be improved and his work more fruitful.*

Article 35 provides that:

> *Each person has the right to personal property and the vital space necessary for the human person to constitute a milieu of liberty and autonomy, with the reservation that this possession not be either a means of oppression or a means of spoiling the legitimate results of the work of others.*

The right to transmit property to one's heirs is also recognized in the declaration. These provisions are included under the Rights of Communities, however, not in the section on the Rights of Persons, thus emphasizing the social nature of property rights.

Part 3 of the personalist declaration relates to the rights

of the state, but refers primarily to limitations on the state. It provides, among other things, that the powers of the state are limited by the powers of the natural societies referred to in part 2 and by fundamental liberties.

While drafting the declaration, Mounier considered the possibility of including a reference to duties in the declaration. Despite his recognition that it is important to link duties to rights from the moral and civic point of view, he concluded that a statement of duties was not acceptable in a legal charter.

In 1789, the drafters of the original French Declaration of the Rights of Man and Citizen, in reaction against orders (clergy, nobility, and commons) in the *ancien régime*, rejected the idea of rights for intermediate groups only the individual had natural rights. But the rights of groups also did not fare well in the revised declaration adopted by the 1946 Constituent Assembly and incorporated as the Preamble to the French Constitution. Only the rights of the family are mentioned in the Preamble. The personalist division of rights into rights of the individual, of groups, and of the state was discussed at length in the Constituent Assembly but eventually was rejected. In the end, not even the right of association was mentioned in the Preamble to the Declaration.

The concept of economic and social rights included in the personalist declaration fared better in the final draft of the French Declaration. Many influences, including Marxist and socialist as well as personalist ones, played a part in the inclusion of these rights in the Preamble. It refers in some detail to the rights workers and other social rights, but includes them in a section labeled "economic and social principles," implying a fundamental difference between them and the liberties included in all earlier part of the declaration. The right to property is also included in the section on "economic and social principles" and emphasizes the social function of all property.

The 1946 French Declaration represents a compromise among competing theories of rights. Jean Rivero, professor of law in Paris, has pointed out that, as a result of the inclusion of economic and social rights in the 1946 Preamble to the Constitution, "human rights no longer have a theoretical unity" in France, adding that what they have lost in theoretical purity, they have gained in scope.

Natural Law, Personalism and Human Rights

Natural law have been linked with conceptions of human rights since the eighteenth century. When the French Declaration of Rights, the Virginia Bill of Rights, and the American Declaration of Independence were drafted, references to the sources of the rights enunciated in these Declarations was not to positive law but rather to the "natural and imprescriptible rights of man," "self-evident" truths, "inherent rights" in short, to natural law concepts. Not all proponents of human rights have been naturalists, but in the absence of a positive law basis for the contention that there are "human rights," an appeal was made to a non positive source and that source was called "natural law." Utilitarian, positivist, and Marxist philosophers reject the natural law basis for human rights; as rights have been progressively included in positive law, both at the national and international level, references to "natural law" have diminished.

In his writings on human rights, Maritain has elaborated a natural law approach to rights that does not coincide entirely with eighteenth century conceptions and not at all with the conservative natural law approaches of the nineteenth- and early twentieth-century judiciary in the United States. Considering that the term has been misused, he, nevertheless, finds no other phrase to replace "natural law":

> *The philosophical foundation of the Rights of Man is Natural Law. Sorry that we cannot find another word. During the rationalist*

> *era jurists and philosophers have misused the notion of natural law to such a degree, either for conservative or for revolutionary purposes, they have put it forward in so over-simplified and so arbitrary a manner, that it is difficult to use it now without awakening distrust and suspicion in many of our contemporaries.*

Maritain's theory of natural law requires explanation since, although it is similar to conceptions of natural law going back to Aristotle, the Stoics, Aquinas, and medieval conceptions, it is not the tradition of natural law best known in the Anglo-Saxon world. Maritain used the terms "personalist" and "humanist" as well as "natural law" to refer to his approach to political organization and rights, and these terms suggest the distinctive elements of his conception of natural law. In distinguishing his approach to rights from that of advocates of a liberal-individualistic approach and of advocates of a communist society, he states that he is an advocate of a personalistic type of society that sees "the mark of human dignity first and foremost in the power to make goods of nature serve the common conquest of intrinsically human, moral and spiritual goods and of man's freedom of autonomy."

Like other naturalists, Maritain bases his conception of natural law on the belief that there is a "human nature" common to all men. The elements of that human nature are simply expressed: man is endowed with intelligence and determines his own ends, which ought to be, but may not be in accordance with his nature. Further, man's knowledge of his "nature" increases "little by little as man's moral conscience has developed." But there is all "immense field of human things which depend on the variable conditions of social life and on the free initiative of human reason, and which natural law leaves undetermined." Maritain's philosophy, though essentialist, has an existential emphasis that recognizes cultural relativity:

> *An immense amount of relativity and variability is to be found in the particular rules, customs, and standards in which, among all*

> *peoples of the earth, human reason has expressed its knowledge even of the most basic aspects of natural law.*

Man is endowed with intelligence and determines his own ends but those deteminations are based on the human situation and "human situations are something existential." While there may be a fundamental nature of man, there is "progress and relativity" regarding human awareness of it.

Maritain's conception of natural Law and rights includes an element of "dynamic development" missing in eighteenth-century, natural law philosophy. Although crediting the eighteenth-century Enlightenment philosophers for developing the concept of rights, he criticizes the resulting catalogue of rights for its rationalism, individualism, and rigidity. It led to a static written code and "ended up, after Rousseau and Kant, by treating the individual as a god and making all the rights ascribed to him the absolute and unlimited rights" of a god. It ignored the social nature of the individual, allowing persons to unfold their "cherished possibilities at the expense of all other beings." Maritain divides his own list of rights into those pertaining to the rights of the human person, the civic person, and the social or working person. He also refers to the rights of economic and social groups to freedom and autonomy. Rights pertaining to the human person include most of the traditional liberties and freedoms of the liberal tradition. Within the category of civic rights, he includes the rights to vote, to have political and legal equality before the law, to enjoy freedom of speech and expression, and to have access to professions without racial or social discrimination. His recognition of social rights is the most distinctive because the eighteenth-century natural-law-based conception of rights has not been congenial to such rights.

Maritain makes a particular contribution to the natural law basis of rights theory by his recognition of the evolutionary nature of concepts of human rights. His listing of rights is based on his own period of time and historical situation, as he emphasizes all catalogues of rights are, but it is doubtful that he would have raised ideological objections to such modern conceptions of rights as the "right to development" and "the right to a clean environment." He writes,

> *We have a tendency to inflate and make absolute, limitless, unrestricted in every respect, the rights of which we are aware, thus blinding ourselves to any other right which would counterbalance them. Thus in human history no "new" right, I mean no right of which common consciousness was becoming newly aware, has been recognized in actual fact without having had to struggle against and overcome the bitter opposition of some "old rights." That was the story the right to a just wage and similar rights in the face of the fight to free mutual agreement and the right to private ownership. The fight of the latter to claim for itself a privilege of divine, limitless absolutism was the unhappy epic of the XIXth Century.*

Maritain recognizes that his natural law conception of the source of human rights is contested by many philosophers and theorists. He refers to the paradox implicit in the effort to find agreement on conceptions of human rights. On the one hand, rational justifications for human rights are indispensable because each person wishes to consent to only what he or she recognizes as true and rationally valid. On the other hand, it is precisely in relation to rational justifications for human rights that we find major disagreements among philosophical traditions. Maritain believed that persons of divergent ideological allegiances, philosophical and religious traditions, cultural backgrounds, and historical experiences could not agree on theoretical conceptions but could agree on a common formulation of practical conclusions, a catalogue of rights. He writes:

> *During one of the meetings of the French National Commission of UNESCO at which the Rights of Man were being discussed,*

> *someone was astonished that certain proponents of violently opposed ideologies had agreed on the draft of a list of rights. Yes, they replied, we agree on these rights,* providing we are not asked why. *With the "why" the dispute begins.*

Maritain was convinced that his way of justifying belief in the "rights of man and the ideal freedom, equality, and fraternity is the only one which is solidly based on truth." His openness to the possibility and even likelihood of agreeing with others on practical action is thus especially striking. In this regard, he underscores the importance of the sociological, rather than the philosophical, point of view:

> *From a sociological point of view, the most important factor in the moral progress of humanity is the experiential development of awareness which takes place outside of systems and on another logical basis at times facilitated by systems when they awaken consciousness to itself, at other times thwarted by them when the obscure the apperceptions of spontaneous reason.*

In focusing on the possibility of agreement on practical action, he states:

> *Thus there is a sort of vegetative development and growth, so to speak, of moral knowledge and moral feeling, which is in itself independent of the philosophical systems, although in a secondary way the latter in turn enter into reciprocal action with this spontaneous process. As a result these various systems while disputing about the "why," prescribe in their practical conclusions rules of behaviour which appear on the whole as almost the same for any given period for culture.*

Roberto Unger's Conception of Rights

Roberto Unger is the best known theorist of the Critical Legal Studies movement (CLS) in North America. That movement has been closely identified with a critique of "rights-talk," the criticism that rights are indeterminate of particular problems and that theories of rights enforce political and social hierarchy.

It may seem surprising, then that Unger has engaged in "rights-talk" and has elaborated a theory of rights supporting his visionary program of "empowered democracy." As Michael Perry and Unger have both pointed out, however, the criticism of rights by some members of the Critical Legal Studies movement has focused not on the conception of rights as such but on particular versions of rights. A valuable contribution has been made by Unger in calling attention to the importance of a conception of rights in any social theory. By a "system of rights" Unger means an institutionalized version of society, which is to say, a form of social life acquiring a relatively stable and delineated form and generating a complicated set of expectations. The stability and the expectations are not merely those of the prison camp: a system of rights defines arrangements that many people treat as the expression of a defensible scheme of human association.

Unger does not draft a declaration of rights in the style of the Mounier personalist declaration. His conception of rights is written in narrative form as an integral aspect of the elaboration of his program of empowered democracy. It is difficult to understand Unger's theory of rights without a detailed understanding of his program of empowered democracy outlined in 653 pages of *False Necessity*. The brief explanation of his conception of rights in this chapter, separated from a lengthy discussion of empowered democracy, risks being inadequate. Even a brief description of Unger's conception of rights, however, will demonstrate how original that conception is, particularly in creating original terminology to refer to various types of rights. His emphasis on concepts of personality and communal life-informs his entire conception of rights.

The distinctive elements in Unger's theory of rights are as follows:

First, Unger rejects the conceptualization of rights as relating solely to relations of the individual *vis-a-vis* the state.

In his conceptualization, rights are relevant to all forms of human association, as he expressed in the following excerpt:

> *Traditional legal thought has accustomed us to think of communal life as almost beyond the proper scope of legal rights. If the jurists are to be believed, legal regulation appears in the domain of intimate and communal relations as the hand of Midas, threatening to destroy whatever it touches. But this supposed antipathy, between rights and community reflects both a rigid view of rights and an impoverished conception of community. Its actual effect is often to leave communal life all the more subject to the forms of self-interested exchange and domination from which the policy of legal abstention as expected to protect it.*

Second, in Unger's conception, rights are not necessarily confrontational. They should nor be seen as "a loaded gun that the right holder may shoot at will at his corner town." Such a concept of rights is incompatible with the give-and-take of a communal vision of society, the necessity, of taking other's situations into account.

Third, Unger writes that our traditional concept of rights is incompatible with the communal vision. Under traditional rights theory, obligations derive either from acts of the will such as bilateral contracts or from state-imposed obligations. But most obligations in ordinary life derive from our relationships of interdependence. Reformed varieties of communal experience, advocated by Unger, "need to be thought out in legal categories and protected by legal rights," which are not the traditional categories of rights.

Fourth, a central aspect of Unger's rights theory is a rejection of what he refers to as the "consolidated property right," the relatively unlimited right to private property of free-market economies. He suggests that the criticism of rights theory by members of the CLS movement have been largely criticisms of the consolidated property right. The consolidated property right has been central to traditional rights theory and has influenced the conception of other rights, but, Unger holds, must be rejected from a personalist and communal view.

Fifth, Unger proposes four kinds of rights to support his personalist and communitarian ideal of empowered democracy: market rights, immunity rights, destabilization rights, and solidarity rights. His concept of market rights is best explained in his own words:

Market rights are the rights employed for economic exchange in the trading sector of the society. They come into their own within a fully realized version of the reconstructed economy: the economy that allows teams of workers, technicians, and entrepreneurs to gain conditional and temporary access to portions of social capital and that thereby develops both the absolute degree of economic decentralization and the extent of economic plasticity.

Such [market] rights would have the basic operational features of contract and property entitlements in current private law. Property, to be sure, would be desegregated, as it has been in so many periods of its history, into a series of distinct powers assigned to different entities or right holders: central representative bodies of the democracy, the competing investment funds, and the capital takers who have access to the fund on explicitly temporary and limited terms.

Unger's concept of immunity rights relates to security for the individual. And by "security" he means the confidence that all individual's physical security, minimal material welfare, and protection against subjugation by public or private power will not be put at risk. He rejects, however, the necessity for private consolidated property rights, lifelong job guarantees, or a particular caste system as means of providing that security. His concept of immunity rights has much in common with traditional liberal civil and political rights but he also includes in this category certain economic and social right. He writes.

Freedom against governmental or private oppression represents only one of two major sets of immunity rights. The other set consists in welfare entitlements: guarantees of access to the material and cultural resources needed to make a life. These include provision for nourishment, housing, health care and education, with absolute standards proportional to the wealth of society.

One of the most unusual aspect of Unger's conception of rights is his category of "destabilization rights." The category is difficult to grasp. He refers to destabilization rights as protecting the citizen's interest in "breaking open the large-scale organizations or the extended areas of social practice that remain closed to the destabilizing effects of ordinary conflict and thereby sustain insulated hierarchies of power and advantage." Unger suggests that these rights may become operational through the arrangements he proposes for empowered democracy; such arrangements have counterparts in the forms of injunctive relief found in contemporary (American) law, as when the courts intervene in institutions like schools or mental asylums or in electoral organization.

Solidarity rights in Unger's conceptualization "give legal form to social relations of reliance and trust." They are intended to support "transformed communal and personal relations" but are not based on altruism or harmony or on a subjective state of mind of the owner of the duty. "Solidarity rights apply to relations within distinct communities and to relations of trust and reliance that take hold outside a well-defined communal setting." Unger points out that the practical legal expression of the view of community underlying the theory of solidarity rights "is the legal protection of claims to abide by implicit obligations to take other people's situations and expectations into account." He cites counterparts in contemporary law supporting his concept of solidarity rights, namely, the law of fiduciary relationships, the contractual and delictual protection of reliance, the doctrines of good faith and of abuse of rights, and the many doctrinal devices by which private law supports communal relations while continuing to represent society as a world of strangers.

Unger admits that solidarity rights may be unenforceable. His treatment of the question of unenforceability provides a summary of his concept of a system of rights:

> *It may be objected that an unenforceable right is no right at all and that merely to speak of such entitlements is to disinter the illogical language of natural rights with its implicit but halfhearted allusion to a natural, absolute context of social life. But it is a mistake to identify, the positivism of governmental enforcement and the idea of innate and eternal entitlements as the only two senses that rights language may bear.*

Not everything in a system of rights need be enforceable, on pain of being treated, if it is unenforceable, as either a natural right or a meaningless gesture. The rights that governmental or other institutions may not enforce remain a public declaration of a public vision, extending, qualifying, and clarifying the ideals embodied in other, enforceable parts of the system of rights.

Sixth, unlike Mounier and Maritain, Unger provides no clear development of group rights. Indeed, in describing market rights, immunity rights, destabilization rights, and solidarity rights, he seems to assume the individual as the right-holder. Nevertheless, his emphasis on the communal nature of society would seem to lead to a conception of the rights of groups as well as individuals. He has not made explicit any such conception of group rights, however.

Similarly to Mounier and Maritain, Unger proposes for our consideration an alternative conceptualization of rights to those we are most familiar with in the West, arguing that some of these alternative views are already implicit in current legal thought and practice.

Summary

The central focus of this chapter has been the cross-cultural implications of personalist perspectives on rights. Personalist-communitarian perspectives on rights, which are becoming increasingly common in the West, more closely approach non-Western conceptions of rights and the conception of rights in the International Bill of Rights.

The great contribution of the Enlightenment philosophers was their concept of individual liberty. But the incorporation of that concept in the French Declaration of the Rights of Man and in the American Declaration of Independence was due as much to felt grievances of the time as to philosophical theories. Today, in the West, the South, the North, and the East, felt grievances continue to include deprivations of personal liberty; but the grievances also relate to economic deprivation and deprivation of the rights of cultural groups. Richard Falk has referred to "intolerabilities" situations that violate elementary principles of humanity and which we cannot accept. The response to such intolerabilities is a conception of rights that relates to them, as the conception of rights of the eighteenth century related to the intolerabilities of that period.

The concept of "rights" is an evolving paradigm. Westerners upholding the traditional liberal concept of "rights" find it conceptually inaccurate to refer to "group rights" or to "economic and social rights." But, as Maritain has pointed out when referring to the term democracy:

> *The choice of words in the practical domain is determined, not by the philosophers, but the usage of men and by the common consciousness. And what matters above all is rediscovering the genuine meaning and value of words charged with great human hopes, and the tone given to their utterance by a conviction based on truth.*

The term "human rights" is now used in non-Western cultures, and increasingly in the West, with content that is not identical with that of Western liberal rights. The political and practical force of human rights rhetoric is available within a personalist perspective in support of contemporary conceptions of human dignity. This chapter has focused on Mounier, Maritain, and Unger, three representatives of a personalist-communitarian approach, because they have provided us with detailed explanations of their conception of rights, which retains a strong emphasis on individual freedoms while including economic rights and group rights. I consider them as representative of a trend in Western rights theorizing. The Catholic bishops of the United States, for example, have called for "a new cultural consensus that the basic economic conditions of human welfare are essential to human dignity and are due persons by right." Whether that consensus is referred to as a "personalist-communitarian perspective" or by some other term is not important. But such a new cultural consensus in the West will have significant cross-cultural implications. Such a perception of rights has much in common with approaches to rights in non-Western countries and the Third World. In addition, it is more fully in harmony with international standards of human rights contained in the Universal Declaration of Human Rights and the two International Covenants on human rights. Mounier, Maritain, and Unger are all contemporary thinkers; as such, they have been influenced by non Western cultural traditions. Maritain was forced to confront his own tradition of rights with that of other cultural traditions during the drafting of the Universal Declaration of Human Rights, and Unger has recognized the influence of the Third World on his conception of politics and social organization. They may be recognized as harbingers of a new theoretical concept of rights, solidly grounded in Western cultural traditions and guarding the best of that tradition, but open to a concept of rights covering the "intolerabilities" of the present age.

6

Problems of Human and Minority Rights

Introduction

More recently the UN General Assembly adopted, in 1992, its Declaration on the Rights of Persons Belonging to National or Ethnic, Religious and Linguistic Minorities. The very adoption of the declaration manifested the increased concern of the United Nations with minority problems, but the title of the declaration indicated the determination of the United Nations to stick to its individualist approach. Article 1 of the declaration, however, says that states "shall protect the existence and the national or ethnic, cultural, religious and linguistic identity of minorities within their respective territories, and shall encourage conditions for the promotion of that identity." This goes further than the previous international law by implying that minorities as such have the rights to state protection of their existence and promotion of their identity. However, it fails to articulate clearly the relations among the rights of individuals and those of minorities.

International law is often unclear because it is the product of political compromises among incompatible positions. Political philosophers can afford to be uncompromising, and therefore should be able to offer clearer accounts of principles that are fudged by international law. Since the lack of clarity in international law, while making agreement on texts possible in the short term, may lay the basis for conflict and injustice in the longer term, we should consider whether political philosophy can provide an analysis of human rights and minority rights that is clear and coherent, and may guide the search for better practical policies.

Problems of Liberal-Democratic Theory

The concept of "human rights" is derived from the tradition of liberal democratic political theory. If we are to find a coherent account of human rights and minority rights, we should expect liberal-democratic theory to provide it. Here we meet our first theoretical problem. We are now so accustomed to associating human rights with liberal democracy, and liberalism with democracy, that we easily forget that rights-liberalism and democracy have had quite different histories and have quite different logics.

We usually trace the concept of "democracy" back to ancient Athens, where it referred to a form of rule, in which "the people" was sovereign. The concept of "democracy" answered two questions, (1) "Who rules?" and (2) "Who ought to rule?" by saying, "the people." It was a class-related concept in that conflicts over who should rule were commonly seen as class conflicts. Class apart, the concept of "democracy" raised no question about culture: it was assumed that, at least for political purposes, "the people" was culturally homogeneous. Athenian democrats also appear to have thought in terms of the duties of citizens rather than of their rights, and certainly lacked the idea of human rights. A similar conception of popular sovereignty was defended in the eighteenth century by Rousseau, who argued that men (I use the word advisedly) could achieve civil liberty only by giving up their natural rights for the rights and duties of citizens, who would make laws for the general good. A free society, in Rousseau's theory, would recognize no conception of human rights (except the right to live in such a free society). As to cultural minorities, either there would be none, or, if they did exist, they would be strictly required to subordinate their culture to the demands of the "general will."

In contrast with the concept of "democracy," rights-liberalism is not primarily concerned with the question of who should rule, but, rather, with what any government, whether democratic or not, may legitimately do and, more particularly, what it may not do. Thus, whereas "democracy" is concerned with the question of who has power, rights liberalism is concerned with the limits of legitimate power, whoever holds it. It is based on the premise that there are certain fundamental human interests or natural rights that derive from human nature and are, in this sense, independent of and prior to society and government. According to John Locke, the first systematic, liberal theorist of rights, natural rights, though deriving their validity from nature (and from nature's God) and not from government, could not be secure in the absence of government and the rule of law because in "the state of nature" there would be sufficient wickedness and self-interest to make men fearful and life inconvenient. All rational persons would, therefore, agree to live under government and law in a society in which public policies were decided by majorities or by the representatives of such majorities. Locke's theory is based on the concept of "natural rights" and derives from that concept a theory of government whose authority depends on the consent of the people and majority rule. Locke did not, however, explicitly require that that government be democratic. His theory also generates no problem of cultural minorities. Minorities are simply a set of individuals who have been outvoted. Such individuals always retain their natural rights and the right to defend them by appropriate means, if necessary, against decisions of majorities that threaten or violate them, but minorities were not seen by Locke as cohesive cultural groups that might need to defend their collective interests against majority tyranny.

Thus both classical liberalism and democratic theory ignored, or were hostile to the idea of, minority rights, but for different reasons. The problematic of liberal theory was the protection of individual freedom from the abuse of power by the state. Such theory assumed the emancipation of the individual from traditional communities and feudal hierarchies; it was consequently silent about the status of cultural minorities, while recognizing the natural rights of their individual members, but was implicitly hostile to them as potential constraints on individual freedom. Democrats, while more "collectivist" than liberals, accorded priority to the political equality of citizens and to the common good and viewed minorities as potential threats to both these values. The "common good" was, classically, that of the *polis* and, in modern times, that of the nation-state, not that of the substate community. Liberal democracy, therefore, seeks to reconcile the liberal values of individual rights and freedoms with the democratic values of citizenship and popular sovereignty. It offers to the members of cultural minorities individual human and citizens' rights, including such rights to collective, cultural life, such as those of freedom of association and religion. Since liberal democracy offers these rights to members of cultural minorities on terms of equality with all other citizens, it considers the status of these minorities within liberal-democratic societies to be, in theory, perfectly just. Actually existing liberal democracies may of course be far from just, but, liberal democrats argue, this is because liberal-democratic principles are often violated in practice. The solution is the robust implementation of the principles, not their abandonment.

The persistence of minority claims in the most "developed" liberal democracies, the established connection between minority problems and the most serious and widespread human rights violations around the world, the articulation of special demands by indigenous peoples, and the end of the Cold War ideological conflict have generated practical and theoretical challenges to this liberal-democratic solution. In response, liberal-democratic theory has reviewed its traditional conceptions of the relations between politics and culture, and between majorities and minorities. The concept of "multiculturalism" has come to occupy a central place in liberal-democratic theory. Liberal-democratic theorists are far from agreement, however, on how liberal democracies should address the problems of multiculturalism. This raises two crucial questions. First, why have liberal-democratic theorists been unable to offer a united front in response to the challenge of multiculturalism? Second, what are the implications of this dissensus for the theoretical status and practical protection of human rights? I shall answer these two questions by analyzing the work of three political theorists, who have proposed powerful versions of different solutions to these problems. Will Kymlicka has developed a theory of minority rights from liberal premises. James Tully has made a more radical critique of liberalism, and argued that it should be replaced by a form of intercultural dialogue. Brian Barry has counterattacked with a robust critique of multiculturalism from a liberal-democratic standpoint. I shall argue that each has advanced our theoretical understanding of minority rights; that each is nonetheless not quite satisfactory; that, although there are significant disagreements among them, they tend to exaggerate their differences; and that a synthesis of their theories is consequently both possible and desirable. The outcome of this analysis is that international law, although not as clear as it ought to be, is basically correct to emphasize the fundamental nature of individual human rights and to incorporate minority rights into the human rights field, but cautiously. This chapter is a vindication of liberal democracy, enriched by the new concerns with multiculturalism and minority rights.

Liberal Theory of Minority Rights

Kymlicka argues that liberalism entails not only the political principles of rights and democracy but also the principle of integration into a particular culture. The liberal concept of national membership that excludes cultural considerations is commonly called "civic" nationalism to distinguish it from illiberal, "ethnic" nationalism. This concept of liberal nationalism is, however, mistaken. What distinguishes "civic" from "ethnic" nations is not the absence of any cultural component of national identity, but, rather, the fact that every citizen can integrate into the common culture without discrimination. In a multicultural society the state necessarily promotes certain cultures and thereby disadvantages others. In a multilingual society, for example, not all languages can be official languages. This raises the question of justice for minorities. This entails, minimally, "the absence of relations of oppression and humiliation between different ethnocultural groups." A more robust concept of ethnocultural justice could, however, be developed by asking what terms of coexistence would be freely consented to by the members of different ethnocultural groups in a setting where inequalities in bargaining power have been neutralized. Liberals assume that people are members of societal cultures, and that these cultures provide the context for individual choice. Liberal states should, therefore, protect this cultural membership. In multinational states, some people's cultural membership can be recognized and protected only by endorsing group differentiated rights.

Yet, Kymlicka argues, all individuals can have experiences that compel them to revise even their most fundamental beliefs. The value of human lives derives not only from their conformity to external standards of the good, but also from the beliefs of the individuals who lead them that they are good. Communities are necessary to good individual lives, but individuals must have some autonomy from the communities of which they are members to choose specific forms of good life. Individuals have autonomy (i.e., the capacity to choose) because community cultures are not homogeneous or fixed. Individuals ought to have autonomy (i.e., the right to choose) because communities can be oppressive. Communities are also often stratified, so that individuals who are required to conform to the demands of "the community" are in reality required to conform to the wills of those with the most power in the community. The defense of group rights may, therefore, be the defense of oppressive power. Liberals therefore cannot approve, except under extreme circumstances, the restriction by minority groups of the basic rights of their members. Liberals believe that individuals should have the capacity and freedom to question the culture of their community, and decide for themselves which aspects of that culture they will retain. Some restrictions on the individual rights of insiders may nevertheless be justified to prevent actions necessary for autonomous choices that would undermine communities. What makes this justification of community restriction of individual rights liberal is that its purpose is to protect a rights-supporting community.

Kymlicka may, by his liberal theory of minority rights, seem to have found a way to reconcile human and minority rights. However, he insists that minority rights cannot be subsumed under the category of human rights. This is not because group rights cannot be human rights, as some human rights theorists argue, but because human rights principles cannot solve some of the most important problems raised by minorities. Some groups are unfairly disadvantaged in the cultural marketplace. The viability of their cultures, for example, may be undermined by political and economic decisions taken by the majority. The members of majority cultures do not face this problem. Given the importance of cultural membership, this is a significant inequality that if not remedied is unjust. The problem with the concept of human rights is not that it necessarily yields the wrong answer to these questions. It is rather that it often gives no answer at all. The right to free speech, for example, does not entail any particular language policy. The principles of human rights leave such matters to majoritarian, democratic decision making, and this may render minorities vulnerable to injustice at the hands of majorities.

Human rights may, however, be insufficient to guarantee even the minimal requirements of ethnocultural justice. Every democratic state has, at one time or another, attempted to create a single national identity among its citizens, and so has tried to undermine any competing national identities, such as those of national minorities. One manifestation of this is the policy of many national governments to encourage people from one part of a country to move into the historical territory of a national minority. Such policies are often designed to exploit the natural resources of the territory and to disempower the national minority by turning them into a minority even in their own traditional homeland. Human rights doctrines, Kymlicka claims, are not only silent on this question, but may exacerbate the injustice because they guarantee freedom of movement within the territory of a state. To protect minorities against this form of oppression, collective rights to land ownership and language use, as well as restrictions on the rights to movement or to vote of the migrants, may be needed. Such group rights are, however, not fundamentally inimical to human rights, for liberal-democratic states claim the right to regulate immigration, land use, and language policies, and such claims are not usually interpreted as threats to human rights. Insofar as such collective rights resemble recognized collective rights of nation-states, they could be subject to the same human rights conditions.

Kymlicka's liberal theory of minority rights has strong implications for education. Liberal societies recognize the right of everyone to freedom of information, including information about ways of life other than their own, and indeed require children to learn about other ways of life, thereby enabling people to revise their beliefs about how to live. Liberal societies do not compel such questioning and revision; they only make it possible. Liberals believe that a person's current way of life is not necessarily the best available, and exposure to other ways of life is necessary for individuals to make informed judgments about which ways of life truly deserve their allegiance. A liberal education, therefore, aims to develop the capacity to evaluate different ways of life. Groups that prevent their members from questioning their culture may thereby be oppressive. Liberals want to protect cultural membership to enable individuals to choose their way of life, and cannot support features of minority cultures that reduce this capacity. There may be inherent value in intergenerational bonds, and parents may have the right to transmit their culture to their children. However, children have the right to information about, and access to, the mainstream culture of the society in which they live, and parents do not have the right to deny this to them.

Kymlicka has been criticized for being a liberal imperialist because he approves of minority groups only if they promote liberal principles. Kymlicka can reply that he is proposing a liberal theory of minority rights. Those who object to liberal principles are not addressing his arguments and should offer their reasons for rejecting liberalism in another context. What concerns us more is the critique that Kymlicka makes of human rights. He has two objections to the idea of human rights in thinking about minorities. The first is that human rights are not sufficient for justice to minorities. The second is that human rights may aggravate injustice to minorities. These objections are easily answered. The answer to the first objection is that Kymlicka is seeking a theory of distributive justice for minorities, and the concept of human rights is not a concept of distributive justice at all but one of minimum standards. Once that elementary point is understood, it is obvious why the idea of human rights is not sufficient for a theory of justice for minorities. Kymlicka's first criticism does not damage the idea of human rights, because it expects of the idea something that it does not claim to provide. The second objection is that the protection of human rights may aggravate injustice by giving members of dominant groups the freedom to oppress and exploit vulnerable minorities. This objection is also based on a misunderstanding of human rights, for it assumes that human rights must be absolute. However, it is a commonplace of human rights theory that human rights may have to be limited for the sake of other, conflicting human rights or of other legitimate values. Article 29, paragraph 2, of the Universal Declaration explicitly provides for this. Thus Kymlicka's liberal theory of minority rights is consistent with the idea of human rights.

Kymlicka seeks to reconcile the liberal theory of justice with the realities of cultural diversity in contemporary societies. Some critics have objected that he achieves this reconciliation only by presupposing the priority of liberal values. Tully seeks to meet this criticism with a theory of politics and culture that presents contemporary societies as a common terrain on which liberalism must come to terms with a "strange multiplicity" of cultures.

Strange Multiplicity

Whereas Kymlicka proposes a liberal theory of minority rights, James Tully criticizes liberal constitutionalism on the ground that it addresses cultural diversity *monologically.* He assumes that cultural diversity is a fundamental feature of the human condition and that cultural recognition is "a deep and abiding human need." The basic institutions and laws of modern societies, and their authoritative traditions of interpretation, are unjust insofar as they fail to recognize cultural diversity but, instead, seek to assimilate or exclude it. Therefore modern, liberal constitutions do not express "popular sovereignty," but are, rather, imperial yokes on culturally diverse citizenries. Tully thus shares with Kymlicka a concern with the political recognition of cultural diversity, but appears to differ from him in seeing liberal constitutions as manifestations of imperialistic oppression.

Culture, Tully maintains, is an irreducible and constitutive aspect of politics. It is a way of interacting with others, and, as citizens interact with each other, so they express their different cultures. Constitutions can impose cultural uniformity or they can recognize culturally diverse ways of being a citizen, but they cannot transcend the cultural dimension of politics. The sovereign people is constituted by its different cultures. A uniform legal and political system, to which all citizens are subject in the same way, denies this cultural diversity unjustly. Most liberal constitutions are unjust in this way. The Canadian Charter of Rights and Freedoms, for example, has been seen as the imposition of a pan Canadian culture. The resistance to liberal constitutionalism by aboriginal peoples, in particular, expresses a refusal of subordinate cultures to accept their roles as passive objects of the dominant culture and a demand for a place in an intercultural dialogue based on mutual recognition of cultures in their own terms. The constitution is, in this view, a continuing intercultural dialogue rather than an original contract or an ideal speech situation.

What are the implications of Tully's critique of liberal constitutionalism for human rights? He says that interculturalism requires "a just form of constitutional discussion in which *each speaker* is given her or his due." This suggests that the recognition of cultural diversity goes all the way down to the level of the individual, and therefore lays the basis for a conception of human rights. The theory is more liberal than it seems: all citizens are equally recognized in terms of their cultural identity. Tully confuses this principle, however, by insisting that the aim of negotiations over cultural recognition is not to reach agreement on universal principles and institutions, but to bring negotiators to recognize their differences and similarities, so that they can reach agreement on a form of association that accommodates their differences in appropriate institutions and their similarities in shared institutions. He does not show why this would not end up with some form of liberal democratic constitutionalism, and it is difficult to understand why we should consider the outcome of such negotiations to be just unless each individual was guaranteed the standard liberal-democratic rights.

Tully rejects any appeal to a transcendental ground of justice beyond the sovereignty of the people, which is defined by thc outcomes of intercultural dialogue. Justice, he maintains, requires the self-government of peoples according to their own cultural understandings. But cultures are overlapping, interactive, and internally negotiated. Consequently cultural difference is internal to particular cultures. Peoples, Tully says, regain "their dignity as equal and active citizens" through self-government. Here he assumes that cultural self-government is compatible with the democratic concept of equal and active citizens. Intercultural constitutionalism appears to be deliberative democracy grounded in a cultural, but also an individualistic, base. The just constitutional recognition and accommodation of cultural diversity, Tully claims, enhances rather than threatens "the primary goods of individual liberty and equality, which are correctly associated with modern constitutionalism, but in a manner appropriate to an age of cultural diversity." The intercultural constitution can reconcile the two goods of freedom and belonging. It can recognize the critical freedom to question in thought and challenge in practice inherited cultural ways and the aspiration to belong to a culture. Here Tully's critique of liberal constitutionalism converges with Kymlicka's liberal theory of minority rights, but it does so by a combination of dialogical justice and the primary goods of freedom and belonging. The coherence of this combination is uncertain, for there is no guarantee that dialogue will produce freedom. Kymlicka may be more of a "liberal imperialist" than Tully, but Tully evades this trap only by qualifying liberal principles with a rather opaque concept of just dialogue. It is not clear whether Tully is really a liberal (and therefore an imperialist in disguise) or really not a liberal (and therefore something unpleasantly illiberal in disguise).

The injustice of constitutional monism, according to Tully, consists in the requirement that cultural minorities converse in the discourse of the dominant group. It stifles cultural differences and imposes a dominant culture while "masquerading" as culturally neutral, comprehensive, or unavoidably ethnocentric. Intercultural dialogue, by contrast, aims to discover which conventions unjustly thwart cultural recognition and which claims to recognition can be shown to be unjust by the conventions that survive the critique. Forms of constitutional recognition that overlook, exclude, or assimilate cultural differences express a residual imperialism that invites the question of its own impartiality as the authoritative language of description and adjudication of claims to recognition. Only a constitutional dialogue in which culturally different ways of participating are mutually recognized would be just, although there must first be agreement on which forms of dialogue are admissible. Tully leaves unclear the criteria that could justly adjudicate the admissibility of forms of dialogue, if liberal-democratic standards cannot be presumed to be impartial. He seeks to reconcile liberal democracy with cultural pluralism, but does not clearly say what justice requires in cases where they are incompatible. Thus he seems to evade the central dilemma of liberal democracy in the face of cultural pluralism.

The institutional form of intercultural constitutionalism is asymmetrical federalism, in which equality is achieved not by the identity of political and legal institutions, but by the equal recognition and autonomy of diverse forms of self-government. Constitutional proposals that affect the individual citizens of the entire federation would require the consent of the majority through their federal representatives or a referendum. Although Tully believes that the political theory of Locke is an example of liberal imperialism, his idea of a federation of cultures rests on a Lockean concept of political society as based on the consent of rights-bearing individuals. Tully holds, however, that the recognition of cultural diversity entails the institution of legal pluralism, which, he claims, is more common in contemporary liberal democracies than liberal-democratic theory itself would suggest.

Despite his polemic against liberal constitutionalism, Tully does not reject liberalism but, rather, seeks to reform it by reconciling it with interculturalism. His theory recognizes dissenting individuals, who are, he acknowledges, more vulnerable because they cannot claim their own political institutions to protect their cultures. The members of minority cultures must seek recognition, accommodation, and affirmation by the majority culture. This invites the question of how conflicts between minority cultures and dissenting individuals should be resolved. Tully admits that legal and political diversity could shield illiberal and undemocratic enclaves; he claims that the consistent application of the conventions of intercultural dialogue would eliminate such enclaves and guarantee the rights of every citizen. When he faces the possibility of the violation of liberal-democratic principles on the ground of cultural diversity, Tully appears to subordinate the diversity to liberal-democratic uniformity.

Cultural diversity is, for Tully, not an alternative to liberal democracy but, rather, a social precondition of one of liberalism's primary goods: individual self-respect. Citizens, he maintains, can take part in popular sovereignty only if they have a certain amount of self-respect. The social bases of this self-respect are the recognition of one's value within shared cultural associations and by outsiders. To provide the social basis for autonomy, therefore, the liberal constitution must protect the diverse cultures in society and promote the public attitude of respect for cultural diversity. Tully's call for cultural recognition for the sake of promoting autonomy makes his argument similar to Kymlicka's. However, it raises the question of the toleration that liberal societies should extend to cultures that do not value autonomy. Kymlicka disapproves of such cultures on liberal grounds, but advocates dialogue between them and liberal cultures. Tully implies support for Kymlicka's solution because the latter advocates intercultural dialogue but analyzes the problem of liberal toleration less clearly.

Although there is a strong liberal-democratic core to Tully's interculturalism, its reliance on dialogue leaves it vulnerable to the same criticism as Kymlicka's theory, namely, that it offers more protection to the powerful than to the weak, and this is unjust. He opposes uniform theories and systems of justice because they are "imperialist" and experienced as oppressive. His alternative is intercultural dialogue, but he wishes to show that this can be validated by liberal-democratic standards of justice, thereby readmitting the universal principles that he has expelled. Tully claims that the constitution of peace and justice can be achieved through intercultural dialogue and not by the imposition of (liberal) Hobbesian sovereignty. He maintains that the imperial, cultural sovereign, even with a liberal face, is responsible both for cultural oppression and the cultural war of all against all. He fails, however, to provide a convincing answer to the hard liberal-Hobbesian question: What if intercultural dialogue delivers neither peace nor (liberal) justice? Tully claims that respect for cultural difference is the guarantee of liberal democracy. Liberal democrats claim that liberal-democratic constitutionalism provides for cultural difference all the guarantees that justice requires. Brian Barry now seeks to dispel the mists of multiculturalism and reaffirm the sufficiency of liberal-democratic justice.

Liberal Democracy vs Multiculturalism

Barry defends a "difference-blind," liberal-democratic concept of justice. He thereby reaffirms the value of impartial justice and opposes Tully's view that liberal justice is imperialism in disguise. Liberal democratic institutions, Barry believes, are both just in themselves and offer the best prospect for just laws and government decisions. Liberalism requires that society accommodate all differences that are compatible with just institutions. It can therefore endorse "difference" provided that it is compatible with liberal-democratic institutions. Liberal democracies treat all citizens as equals: no individual or group is considered to have less intrinsic worth than others, and no individual or group may be arbitrarily privileged. A liberal state should take strong measures against harassment and discrimination. However, no society can tolerate all difference, since some social practices are unacceptably harmful to others and to society. If liberal democracy is to flourish, its citizens must be committed to its core values: liberal democracy cannot, and should not, tolerate those who would undermine it. Such toleration would be unjust. In contrast to Tully Barry opposes the delegation of responsibility for public services to communal groups. He believes that this tends to ghettoize minorities and leaves them more vulnerable to the dominant groups in the larger society. Participation in common institutions creates solidarity, which is the best protection for minorities. Liberal democracy depends upon civic nationalism.

Both Kymlicka and Tully would object to Barry's defense of "difference-blind" liberal democracy that liberal states cannot be culturally neutral, and that, consequently, supposedly impartial, "difference-blind" justice conceals the unjust domination of particular cultures. "Civic" nationalism is always biased by forms of ethnic stratification that are the products of historical injustices. The dominant national culture often includes a sense of superiority to other cultures even when it endorses liberal-democratic institutions. To become "citizens," members of subordinate ethnic groups must give up significant elements of their culture and adopt the culture of the historically dominant group. The public culture of liberal-democratic, civic nationalism, in this view, requires the marginalization of rival ethnic cultures. Against this critique of civic nationalism it may be urged that its record of protecting ethnic minorities is impressive. For example, Helen Fein has argued on the basis of a detailed empirical analysis that Jewish chances of survival during the Holocaust were considerably higher in those countries occupied by the Nazis in which civic nationalism was greater. Denmark is only the best known example of this general truth. There is, therefore, empirical evidence to support both the case of Kymlicka and Tully, on the one hand, and that of Barry, on the other, with regard to the record of civic nationalism in protecting minorities.

Barry is uncompromising in refusing to tolerate the devolution of political power to illiberal cultural groups, and he finds both Kymlicka and Tully too compromising on this point. Liberal toleration of illiberal groups that do not exercise devolved political power depends, he believes, on the right to exit. The liberal dilemma is that liberals are committed to freedom of association, but they must also limit their toleration of groups' oppression of their own members. Barry seeks to resolve this dilemma by clarifying the principle of freedom of association. He argues that if the members cannot leave or if the cost of exit is unreasonably high, then the association is not "free," and consequently not protected by liberal principles. What makes the cost of exit unreasonably high? Barry suggests that the cost of losing the benefits of membership by exit does not render an association involuntary, because such a cost is inherent in any exit and is therefore entailed by the principle of freedom of association. However, if the association threatened, harassed, or penalized the departing member that would be unreasonable, and might mean that the association was not voluntary. Among the costs of exit from a "comprehensive" community in which, for example, religion and economy are closely integrated may be loss of capacity to earn a living. In such cases, Barry thinks, the leaver may have not a right to remain, but a publicly enforceable right to compensation. The test of a "reasonable" cost of exit is not the suffering of the leaver, but the rights of the association. A voluntary association has the right to insist that its members adhere to its beliefs and conform to its rules, and those who choose to leave because they change their "conception of the good" have no grounds for legitimate complaint, even if they are very sad to leave the group. A voluntary religious group is, therefore, not required to tolerate dissenters, but the group may not harass them, and, if the dissidents are economically dependent on the community, the group may be obliged to compensate them.

The liberal state, in Barry's theory, is not to impose any way of life on any of its citizens. He criticizes Kymlicka for requiring that minorities should promote "autonomy." Thus, he holds that Kymlicka is not only insufficiently liberal because he would tolerate illiberal groups, but also guilty of "liberal imperialism" for seeking to impose an autonomous way of life on groups that do not value it. Barry's criticism of Kymlicka is inaccurate, however, for Kymlicka is only defending the equal right to liberty that Barry also defends. "Autonomy" in Kymlicka's theory is not a "way of life" but the right to change one's way of life. It is a liberal principle, and Barry should not oppose it.

For Barry, liberalism is universalistic. Nobody, anywhere in the world, should be denied protection against injustice and oppression. However, although liberalism is universalistic in principle, the question of intervention may be answered on pragmatic grounds. Barry strongly criticizes Kymlicka's reluctance to endorse forceful intervention by liberal states in illiberal communities. Kevin Dwyer has argued, along much the same lines as Barry, that Kymlicka's theory itself justifies state enforcement of gender equality in education against the will of recalcitrant cultural minorities, for minorities' claims to recognition, self-respect, and equality can all be transferred to support a robust public policy of gender equality in education. Also, because his grounding value is autonomy, Kymlicka should be less concerned with the rights of minorities and more with the rights of children. However, insofar as the question of intervention is a matter for pragmatic judgment, the difference between Barry and Kymlicka may not be as great as Barry believes. Kymlicka's judgment is informed by the persistent failure of liberal states in their policies toward aboriginal peoples and ethnic minorities, whereas Barry draws a sharper distinction between liberal principle and prudent practice. This distinction makes for clear thinking. There is, however, a reason of principle for caution about intervention that plays a role in Kymlicka's thought. The agents of the liberal state who intervene in minority ways of life for the sake of liberal principles may be insensitive to the value of such ways of life to the members of the minority. They may be what Eamonn Callan calls "liberal Jacobins." Barry might consider this argument to be merely pragmatic or covered by the principle of freedom of association. There is, however, an argument of principle that self-emancipation is, all other things being equal, better than liberation from outside. All things, of course, rarely are equal, but that is a pragmatic consideration. There are, therefore, principles and pragmatic considerations that may be invoked both for and against liberal intervention in the practices of illiberal groups.

Tully argued that public recognition of the diverse cultures in society is necessary to the self-respect of the members of subordinate cultures, which is in turn necessary to liberal democracy. Barry objects to this argument because he believes that Tully is committed to the view that "culture" provides a moral justification for a social practice. Barry holds that the goodness and badness of cultural practices must be judged by criteria other than the mere fact that they are cultural practices. If this were not so, the Nazis could have justified their anti Semitism on the grounds that it was a well-established feature of German culture. No one, according to Barry, has the right to be respected solely on the basis of their culture because no one has a duty to respect culture as such. The only sort of respect for others required by liberal-democratic principles is the recognition that everyone is an equal citizen irrespective of their cultural commitments.

However, Barry misses the main point of Tully's case for the political recognition of subordinate cultures. This does not require us to respect cultures that do not deserve respect from a liberal point of view (although Tully does not, it is true, always make this clear). It requires us to acknowledge that certain cultures have been despised historically and that the failure to remedy the legacy of this history undermines liberal-democratic equality. Charles Taylor has pointed out that modernization, including liberalization, can be experienced by some cultural groups as "engulfment" and imperialist imposition. Cultural assertiveness can be an expression of dignity. This assertiveness may appear as the defense of conservative against liberal values, but in historical context it can also be a claim for equality against domination. Barry defends a rather historical liberalism. Recognition theorists believe that actual liberalism has a historical record of oppression. The political recognition of minorities and aboriginal groups is an attempt to rectify unjust, historical domination. Unfortunately, neither Tully nor Taylor makes it clear that this call for cultural recognition rests on liberal principles. Barry's liberalism has the virtues of clear and robust principles. What it lacks, and Tully provides, is empathy with subordinated cultures. Those who have been despised need (and have the right) to be respected not only as citizens but in order to be citizens. This entails public recognition of the cultures that constitute their identities, although this recognition must be conditioned by the requirements of liberal-democratic justice, for it is the latter that justifies the call for recognition.

Barry accepts that cultural differences will persist because there will necessarily be differences of opinion about which is the best way to live, and there is no known method of resolving such disagreements. The human condition is, however, sufficiently uniform to claim plausibly that every society must achieve certain standards to provide a decent life for all its members. Moreover, the very fact of irresolvable disagreement over the nature of the good life, once we get beyond the basics, is itself a premise of the argument for liberal institutions, for, in the face of these disagreements, what we need is a fair way of adjudicating between the conflicting demands that the institutions give rise to. That is what liberal democracy offers.

The case for liberal democracy rests on this combination of the universal nature of the "basics" and irreducible disagreement about the rest. Barry defends a version of universal human rights and is suspicious of, or downright hostile to, minority rights that go beyond or, worse, threaten to undermine human rights. Kymlicka argued that human rights were insufficient for justice and might sometimes aggravate injustice. We have seen, however, that his critique of human rights is weak, since human rights principles specify minimum standards and not a theory of distributive justice, and human rights must be limited for the sake of rights and other values. The difference between Kymlicka and Barry on minority rights is not as great as Barry suggests, because Kymlicka's theory is motivated by liberal principles. Whether it is well designed to implement those principles depends in part on complex empirical considerations, especially about the consequences of intervention. Tully proposed intercultural dialogue in place of liberal constitutionalism, but defended the plausibility of his proposal by requiring that the dialogue meet liberal-democratic criteria. He too does not reject human rights—although he does not clearly affirm them but appears to go further in defending minority rights. This appearance is, however, subverted by his concept of "strange multiplicity," which calls into question the homogeneity of the minorities to which rights might be ascribed.

Barry disputes Kymlicka's claim that there is an emerging liberal consensus on minority rights. There is, however, more agreement than appears on the surface. Barry's civic nationalism and liberalism may appear "imperialistic" and "monological" from Tully's perspective, but they permit all cultural practices that are not illiberal and some illiberal practices in private groups that recognize a right of exit. Tully's intercultural alternative cannot be very tolerant of illiberal practices, since its rationale is the condemnation of unjust domination. Kymlicka argues that civic nationalism without minority rights is unjust among cultural groups, but minority rights are intended to strengthen, not challenge, liberal-democratic justice. Barry concedes that there may be pragmatic arguments for minority rights, so even here the difference may not be great. There are two interrelated weaknesses in Barry's otherwise strong argument for liberal democracy. The first is the underestimation of the impact of historical injustice on the distribution of "primary goods" in the present. The second is the importance of public respect for cultural groups as a requirement of equal citizenship. For these reasons a synthesis of these three theories may be both possible and desirable. None is quite right. Together they have most of the ingredients of the best available theory of liberal-democratic justice and minority rights.

Summary

The idea of minority rights is older than that of human rights, and emerged from the religious divisions of the Reformation, the development of the Westphalian state system, and the rise of religious toleration. It was, however, rooted in premodern communal ways of life. The idea of human rights expressed the emancipation of individuals from communal ties as well as the need to protect them from oppressive states. This liberal individualism was attacked both by conservative and socialist communitarians. History does not, however, leap with a single bound from premodern communitarianism to modern individualism. Liberalism always presupposed a nationalist framework. In the aftermath of World War I there was an attempt both to affirm the liberal principle of national self-determination and the rights of minorities. This attempt failed, and was exploited by Nazi Germany with terrible consequences that are well known. Consequently, when the United Nations sought to establish a new world order after World War II the idea of minority rights was discredited, and the liberal, individualist conception of human rights predominated.

The idea of human rights proved hard to implement partly because violations of human rights were protected by the doctrine of state sovereignty and partly because the Cold War made the political implementation of human rights extremely difficult. However, problems of minorities persisted even in countries in which human rights were relatively well respected. The worldwide struggle against imperialism inspired movements of political and cultural protest by minorities and indigenous peoples in liberal-democratic societies. The political philosophy of liberal democracy was slow to recognize the problem. John Rawls's theory of justice is paradigmatic of this failure. Significantly, Kymlicka's influential liberal theory of minority rights is based on revising Rawlsian liberalism by adding a cultural dimension. Tully appears to challenge liberalism more directly, but, on close inspection, his dialogical interculturalism is another formulation of multicultural liberalism. Barry reaffirms a quasi-Rawlsian liberalism with the depoliticization of culture. In so doing he is reaffirming Mrs. Roosevelt's view that the effective implementation of human rights would be sufficient to protect the legitimate interests of minorities.

The recent debate in political philosophy has advanced our understanding of the place of cultural minorities in liberal democracies. But it has suffered from an excessively polemical style. Tully, for example, attacks liberal constitutionalism but defends a *form* of liberal constitutionalism. Barry offers a critique of multiculturalism but defends liberal democracy partly on the ground that it provides a generous space for multiculturalism. What are the practical implications of the debate? To answer this question clearly, we have to make two second-order theoretical distinctions. The first is that between history and theory. The second is that between theory and practice. Barry believes that political theory is not a historical discipline, because history produces good and bad, and only an historical theory can distinguish between the two. Kymlicka and Tully rely on history to show that liberal impartiality and civic nationalism are unjust unless rectified by minority rights or intercultural dialogue. The two apparently contradictory positions can be reconciled if we identify the level of abstraction at which they are properly applicable. At a certain, rather high level of abstraction Barry is right, and this is shown by Tully's failure to produce criteria for his distinction between admissible and inadmissible dialogue. This would require precisely the kind of a historical theory that Barry defends. However, at a more concrete level the kind of historical facts to which Kymlicka and Tully appeal become morally relevant. Given, for example, that imperialism stands condemned as unjust at the bar of liberal justice, actual liberal societies have an obligation to rectify the legacies of imperialism. This may require some form of minority rights or intercultural dialogue.

This leads to the distinction between theory and practice. Barry believes, on the basis of liberal-democratic principles, that Kymlicka concedes too much to illiberal minorities. He acknowledges, however, that there may be pragmatic limits to interventions by liberal states. Kymlicka and Tully believe that Barry's form of liberal democracy ignores the realities of ethnocultural inequalities. It is not clear whether the difference between Barry and Kymlicka is one of principle or of practical judgment. There does appear to be a difference of principle between Barry's impartialist, "monological" conception of justice and Tully's dialogical conception. On close inspection, however, the difference is blurred and probably smaller than it seems. Barry's theory has the considerable merit of clearly stating the principles of liberal democracy. Pragmatic judgment is by its nature less clear-cut. Some of the differences between Barry, on the one hand, and Kymlicka and Tully, on the other, lie on the boundary between theoretical principle and pragmatic judgment. This boundary is difficult to lay down very clearly.

Liberal-democratic theory has of course never been uniform. Utilitarian liberals, for example, rejected the idea of natural rights, and Kantians reject utilitarianism. It is, therefore, not surprising that the question of multiculturalism and minority rights should produce different responses from liberal democrats. This is even less surprising when we recall that liberal democracy has historically, both in practice and in theory, taken culture for granted. The cultural critique of traditional liberal-democratic theory draws much of its force from the critique of imperialism. This is particularly apparent in the work of Tully. However, Tully himself indicates, and Barry emphasizes more strongly, that anti-imperialism can conceal oppression and injustice within cultural groups. The oppressed can themselves be oppressors. Barry argues robustly that the appeal to cultural autonomy without respect for human rights is incoherent and morally repulsive. In defending "difference blind" liberal democracy, however, Barry underestimates precisely what Kymlicka and Tully emphasize: the imperialist ghost in the liberal-democratic machine. Contemporary liberal democracy can, and should reach out sympathetically to cultural minorities that have been historically oppressed without betraying its own principles. This is often difficult both in theory and in practice. In deciding exactly which rights, if any, minorities should have, theory can only lay down general guidelines and then hand over policymaking to practical judgement. Although the international law of human rights is confused, and political theory can clarify the principles that should underlie it, it is not mistaken to have moved into the field of minority rights with great caution. The protection of the rights of minorities does not require a lot of law. It requires clear principles, much goodwill, and considerable courage. It requires above all what philosophy has traditionally promised but, alas, rarely delivered: wisdom.

7

Human Rights and Political Values in East Asia

Introduction

Constitutionalism is usually understood to include three core components: democratic elections with multiparty competition; security of human rights, including freedom of expression; and the rule of law with firm adherence to principles of legality. To these core components I add a fourth ingredient, the local institutional embodiment that connects constitutional government to the local condition, what I call *indigenization.*

Given the enormous power that modern states have, theorists have often focused on the constraints constitutionalism imposes on the state. While appreciating concerns with constraint, I emphasize, instead, the positive discourse-engendering role of constitutionalism. Through constitutionalism the state provides the political and legal architecture of a contemporary commitment to human rights and the venue for the contemporary discussion of cultural-political values and development. In relation to human rights, the compelling task is to show how constitutional institutions with appropriate local extensions can best address various concerns raised in the Asian values and developmental debates.

At the same time it is important to consider how constitutionalism offers a venue that can serve the local community in its interactions with the international human rights debate. The argument in this chapter proceeds in two major parts by considering, first, the various claims on behalf of authoritarianism made in the name of cultural-political values and development, and, second, how constitutionalism, through its core components and its local institutional embodiment (indigenization), works to construct a venue for an open-ended conversation about political values and development. It is important to remember that domestic constitutional systems provide the primary venues for the global human rights debate. Such local venues allow for a degree of diversity in human rights practice.

East Asian Human Rights Debate

Here I wish to address several prominent authoritarian-based arguments made on behalf of cultural values and economic development, including, first, the specific Asian values claims on a substantive level; second, a related cultural prerequisites argument that seeks to disqualify some societies from realization of democracy and human rights; third, claims made on behalf of community or communitarian values in the East Asian context; and, fourth, the argument that seeks justification for authoritarianism in East Asia's historical record of rapid economic development. While the first three of these relate more directly to cultural values, the fourth combines such values with authoritarian developmentalism. The latter also considers the implications of the East Asian economic crisis that began in the late 1990s. Taken as a whole, this analysis offers a challenge to claims made on behalf of authoritarian regimes and sets the stage for the discussion of constitutionalism in the remainder of this chapter.

Authoritarian Claims about Asian Values

Focusing on political values and confining this discussion mainly to the East Asian Confucian context, the main substantive claim is that Asian values are antidemocratic and hostile to liberal protection of human rights. Asian societies are said to favor authority over liberty, the group over the individual, duties over rights, and such values as harmony, cooperation, order, and respect for hierarchy. Emphasizing these characteristics, East Asian supporters of authoritarianism have argued that their societies are unsuited to democracy and human rights. That these claims are usually made on behalf of authoritarian leaders raises suspicion about the honesty of the claims. On a substantive level, these claims are challenged both by the rapid recent development of democracy and human rights in several East Asian societies and by social activist and scholarly discourses that challenge such claims directly. The growing consolidation of democracy in East Asia largely speaks for itself. Former authoritarian systems, including those in Japan, South Korea, Taiwan, the Philippines and, to some extent, Hong Kong, Indonesia, and Thailand, have all undergone recent democratic reform. Even though each of these systems continue to be plagued with vestiges of authoritarianism, the reformist direction is clearly evident and indicates a serious concern about democracy and human rights in East Asian societies.

Direct attacks on the intellectual foundations of the Asian values claim have also been launched by activists and analysts, challenging several of the claim's components. Regarding the association of Confucianism with authoritarianism, Chinese scholars of the Confucian classics have noted (1) that Confucianism did not embrace unquestioning acceptance of misguided rule and (2) that it shares with liberalism the commitment to higher norms. Confucian scholar Chang Wejen especially points out the prominent position of the golden rule in Confucian ethics. Chang notes that the harsh practices of the late dynastic cycle, sometimes known as neo-Confucianism, were more a product of dynastic rule and Chinese legalism than they were of traditional Confucian thought. Other scholars have challenged the motives of those who advance the above stereotypes concerning Asian values. Edward Said long ago noted that Western "orientalism" offered up its conception of Asia as "the other" in part to justify Western dominance. More recently, other Asian scholars have noted the tendency of East Asian leaders and scholars to adopt orientalism as a self-defining discourse. The same conception that aimed at Western dominance now, in East Asian authoritarian hands, aims at creating East Asian exceptionalism.

Another line of reasoning would have us believe that East Asian intellectuals did not understand Western liberal democracy when first confronted with it in the early modern period. In the Chinese context, this was said to produce a perverse reinterpretation that saw democracy as merely good government or social welfare, in line with the Chinese *minben* (people as a basis) tradition. There is no doubt that authoritarian reinterpretations did occur and that Chinese nationalism, especially following the May 4th Movement, did produce a distorted understanding. But recent studies of early modern Chinese writings witness a great deal of understanding of leading Western liberal thinkers. Other Asian scholars and specialists have pointed out that much of what is done in the name of so-called authoritarian Asian values can be explained more often than not by expediency. Frequently this expediency is accompanied by other ideological constructs, such as Marxism, that have little to do with Asian traditions. Francis Fukuyama argues that the only neo Confucian authoritarian system evident in recent East Asian experience was the government of prewar Japan.

Cultural Prerequisites

My second critique relates to the claim that societies lacking certain cultural prerequisites are not suited for democracy and human rights. This notion has its roots in studies that sought to examine the characteristics of civic culture that exist in Western democracies. These studies clearly were not aimed at supporting cultural relativist arguments. In comparative studies of political development and democratization this hopeful line of reasoning, however, became burdened with the pessimistic view that societies that lacked civic culture were not likely to be successful at democratization. It was as if societies had to pass a test for democracy. This scholarship could lend further support for authoritarian Asian values reasoning: societies burdened with authoritarian Asian values may be judged poor soil for democracy and the concomitant values associated with human rights and the rule of law.

But the problems with this reasoning are apparent. The most obvious is its tautological character. To suggest that a society that lacks democracy could somehow develop democratic culture is a questionable proposition. The fact is that many societies in East Asia proceeded with democratization, with or without the allegedly required civic culture. With democratic institutions in place, the emphasis has shifted to consolidation and to creating the institutions to make democratization work. Nevertheless, scholars and politicians in East Asia have sometimes clung tenaciously to this claim concerning prerequisites. The task of documenting the presence of civic culture in East Asia still contributes to a mindset that appears to conceive of a test for democratization. This has spawned a persistent argument by those in some communities who oppose democratic reform, saying that the local society is not yet ready for democracy.

Claims about Community

My third critique considers a more consciously intended cultural relativist argument, and one that is to some extent more credible. This is the one made on behalf of community. This argument fails to justify the denial of democracy and human rights, but it does raise some concerns that I argue in the next part of this chapter must be addressed by societies hoping to better secure human rights. There are essentially three community-based arguments addressed here. The first is the romanticization of community. The Vietnamese village, for example, has been described as "anchored to the soil at the dawn of History behind its bamboo hedge, the anonymous and unseizable retreat where the national spirit is concentrated," while the Russian *mir* was to "save Russians from the abhorrent changes being wrought in the West by individualism and industrialization." Many have questioned just how liberating the traditional village was, and many escaped when they had the chance. Few in East Asia's diverse urban economies have the option of unmolested village life today.

Another community-based claim, one emphasizing republican government and civic virtue, has ancient roots and is of contemporary interest. In many East Asian societies civic virtue is seen as the key to good government. The debate over civic virtue, an ancient philosophical concern, has persisted on a global scale throughout the modern period of democratization. But many democratizers, in practice, have not been confident of the persistence of civic virtue and have sought to craft a democracy that, in James Madison's terms, is safe for the unvirtuous. The debate in the Czech Republic between Vaclav Havel, the anticommunist idealist who has emphasized civic virtue, and Vaclav Klaus, the pragmatic postcommunist politician who is more concerned with interest representation, is likely to be rehearsed in postcommunist and post authoritarian East Asia. As has been true in other parts of the world, civic virtue alone will not likely be enough; nor will its persistence be reliable.

A third community-based claim, communitarianism, offers the centrality of community as an alternative to liberal individualism. Communitarianism is the most challenging contemporary discourse about community. There is, however, a wide gap between the Western and the more prominent forms of East Asian communitarian perspectives. While Western communitarians are apt to see community as a venue for democratic discourse and liberation, the neoconservative brand of so-called communitarianism evident in Singapore is hardly a venue for democracy and liberation. In this East Asian variant "communitarianism" has generally meant authoritarianism, as the regime seeks to implant its value system, emphasizing a conservative version of "Asian values" and passive acceptance of the regime's dictates. Western communitarians have often felt the need to be committed to some liberal values to preserve their discourse and overcome some less acceptable values associated with traditional communities, while the Asian neoconservative variety has also had to deal with increased demands for liberalization. In both cases, those committed to addressing communitarian concerns are likely to be left to determining how to deploy some liberal institutions in ways that are responsive to these concerns.

Economic Development

Until recently, the seeming most compelling East Asian argument on behalf of authoritarianism has been the one in support of the East Asian model of economic development. Authoritarian leaders in East Asia have argued that authoritarianism, under a developmentally-oriented political elite, can allow for stability and long-term predictability.

According to this East Asian view, export-led growth combined with micro planning of industrial development led to the developmental successes sometimes characterized as the East Asian "economic miracle." Such an East Asian model is said to be typified by the Japanese developmental model of the 1960s and 1970s, and was evident in similar success stories in South Korea, Taiwan, and Singapore. Under such systems, without the perceived burdens of democracy and rights, excessive public welfare-oriented expenditure, sometimes characterized as rent seeking, could be avoided. Under the Japanese model an elite coalition of the leading political party, bureaucracy, and business is said to have allowed government institutions charged with industrial and trade policy to operate effectively. Such bureaucratic institutions are said to be both autonomous and, to a degree, embedded, facilitating a satisfactory process of developmentally-oriented central planning. Under this system, authoritarian interventions aim to ensure high levels of productive investment, reduced labor cost through select welfare subsidy and labour suppression, fast transfers of technology, targeting of key industries, and substantial international competitiveness. The targeting of key industries was especially achieved through political and bureaucratic interference in the targeting of industrial loans for select industries.

Until the 1990s these arguments seemed compelling, as the East Asian "tiger" economies grew at unprecedented rates. This high growth rate extended beyond the five leaders to capitalist economies in Southeast Asia and to economically reforming China. But in the 1990s the economic crisis, first in Japan and then in the late 1990s elsewhere in the region, called this model into question, as extensive evidence of corruption and cronyism emerged. In many respects the very mechanisms that facilitated growth, through key industry targeting, produced corporate debt overhang that exacerbated the financial crisis that followed.

The existence of democratic institutions may have determined not only who felt the worst effects of the crisis, but also those likely to more quickly rebound. Of the three countries hit first with the financial crisis, Indonesia, then the least democratic, was hit the hardest. Democracies, such as Taiwan, faired better, and even among those countries hit hard by the crisis the more democratic ones, such as South Korea and Thailand, have appeared to bounce back more quickly. Scholars who have studied the relative capacity of democracies and authoritarian regimes in dealing with economic crisis or shocks have come out strongly in favor of democracy. Dani Rodrik notes that economic shocks will generally be worse in societies with deep latent conflicts and argues that democracy "affords the ultimate institutions of conflict management." In reference to the current East Asian economic crisis, Donald Emmerson argues that East Asian countries with high levels of political freedom have been generally more resilient. In the South Korean case, voters quickly replaced the leadership more closely associated with the former authoritarian regime, electing Kim Dae-jung to the presidency. Because of a political coalition with strong labor support, Kim has shown a willingness and some ability to gain popular support for the hard restructuring decisions he has had to make. The importance of democracy in facilitating development and dealing with economic shock has not, however, been apparent to all. Hard-line governments such as those in China, Vietnam, Burma, Malaysia, and Singapore still cling to hope for sustaining authoritarian or quasi authoritarian development with high economic growth.

In the 1990s, theorists continued to laud the achievements of the East Asian model while recommending adjustments. Some promoted a kind of liberal authoritarianism, others promoted illiberal democracy. The notion of liberal authoritarianism aims to preserve the best qualities of the East Asian model while ensuring the rule of law, thereby reducing corruption and cronyism. But as Jon

Elster rightly points out, the problem is that a dictator "is unable to make himself unable to interfere with the legal system whenever it becomes expedient." At the other extreme, illiberal democracy would preserve the East Asian model of consensus and control along with some degree of democratization. With democratization such authoritarian economic models did indeed persist in several leading economies. The persistence of cronyism and corruption evident in the economic crisis of the late 1990s tended to call this model into question. Furthermore, it is doubtful whether democratic leaders without modern constitutional institutions to check their power will remain democratic. At the turn of the century, the continuing economic crisis has brought an increasing urgency to this discussion.

At the present stage, a more realistic conclusion is that just tinkering with this East Asian model is not sufficient. In my view, it is not so much that the model was from the start totally flawed as that it is a victim of its own success. The economic deprivation in the East Asian region at the start of its developmental phase allowed authoritarian governments that could deliver the goods to survive with little contest. But with success, the level of diversification of interests in these rapidly developing economies increased dramatically. Increased social complexity and stratification are likely to overtax authoritarian institutions. Tracing causal mechanisms, Dietrich Rueschemeyer, Evelyne Stephens, and John Stephens argue that the case for liberal democracy becomes compelling at a certain point in the industrialization process because industrialization and economic development transform society to empower subordinate classes. Under these conditions, three causal factors may point to the need for change: first, higher expectations among middle and subordinate classes and other social interest groups produce increased demands for participation; second, rapid economic expansion makes both the likelihood and the costs of corruption intolerable; and, third, economic restructuring and globalization encourage a national consensus-building process to avoid massive social disruption.

In East Asia this evolutionary process has been evident in recent years. The basis for change is increasingly apparent. Without political reform, the channels of representation of the diverse interests in these rapidly developing societies became clogged. In the late 1980s, the increase in reported cases of corruption throughout the region seemed to suggest that in the absence of reform, corruption had become the channel to get things done. As the scale of both growth and corruption increased, so did the public dissatisfaction with the latter. Economic elites also appeared to be less compliant as they become more globally competitive. In the most developed countries of the region, it appears that increased wealth and education led middle and various subordinate classes to demand greater participation, openness, and accountability. These developments were evident in Taiwan, South Korea, and Japan in the late 1980s. Labor and student unrest and the mass *minjung* movement eventually toppled the South Korean regime, which seemed compelled to accept political reform. In Taiwan a middle-class push for democracy achieved success with an increasingly compliant regime, ultimately leading to democratization. In Japan, the struggle over corruption produced increased public scrutiny and pressure for liberalization. A similar stage soon may be reached in China, where the reform of the state enterprise system will certainly increase pressures from social unrest. With the incentives for economic and political reform in place, democratization and reform has increasingly been the norm of the most successful East Asian economies. I argue next that these developments favour a form of liberal constitutionalism.

Constitutionalism

Constitutionalism offers a venue to respond to the various claims underlying the cultural values and developmental debates and a response to those who advance authoritarianism as a venue for addressing such concerns. The concept of constitutionalism I advance includes the fundamental elements of democracy, human rights and the rule of law, and elements of local institutional embodiment, or what I call indigenization. At the dawn of the twenty-first century the discussion of constitutionalism has become a global conversation, a conversation that is productive of the processes of universalizing human rights. Constitutionalism serves both as a conduit for shared international and local human rights and political values and the embodiment of those values. In this regard, the following sections emphasize two aspects of the constitutional equation: first, the empowering role of constitutionalism, in contrast to the usual view that emphasizes only constraint; and, second, indigenization of constitutionalism, as a conduit to hook it up to the local condition, in service of both values and economic development. All these aspects have been implicated in the East Asian debate over political reform and liberalization.

Empowering Role of Constitutionalism

Some theorists have worried that constitutionalists place too much emphasis on the constraints of constitutionalism, always using language of "checking, restraining or blocking." Emphasis on constraint may cause constitutionalists to overlook the important empowering aspects of constitutionalism. Here, it is important to stress that the idea of constraint through human rights has been important and remains so due to the enormous power of the state in the modern period. Such power was even further enhanced under the influence of nineteenth-century legal positivism and its ideas of sovereign exclusivity. But the notion of constraint under constitutional government takes on meaning and force only through popular empowerment. Under constitutional government, the processes of empowerment extend beyond the institutions of electoral politics to include the processes of human rights and the rule of law. It is the integration of political and legal institutions in the processes of constitutional government that allows empowerment and constraint to work.

It is therefore important to emphasize the positive empowering role of constitutionalism. The notion of a self-imposed constraint is a questionable proposition in a world where leaders frequently ignore constraints. This is important because under this constraint paradigm, newly elected democratic leaders may view it as part of their mandate to override constraint to "get the job done." This may result in what Guillermo O'Donnell calls "a caesaristic plebiscitarian executive that once elected sees itself as empowered to govern the country as it deems fit. " East Asia has in recent years experienced the phenomenon of the powerful state and the hazard of unconstrained government, elected or otherwise. The most notorious East Asian examples where elected leaders used their mandate to pervert the constitutional order were some of the early South Korean experiments with democracy and the Marcos regime in the Philippines.

In East Asia, as already noted, theorists have responded with two nearly opposing alternatives, often paradoxically applied to the same regimes. Some have advocated instituting the rule of law and rights protection along with authoritarianism. The difficulty with this option is inducing such authoritarian leaders to consistently accept such constraint. There have been some aspirations toward this notion in Singapore, Malaysia, and (until recently) Indonesia. Alternatively, some may advocate instituting democracy but replacing liberal constraints with alleged East Asian cultural constraints and communitarian processes of bargaining. Paradoxically, this may be the aspirational basis of the claims to democracy made by the same regimes in Singapore, Malaysia, and Suharto's Indonesia. But an alleged democracy without core constitutional constraints, that prohibits or suppresses opposition, does not appear to be democracy at all. A system that places emphasis on social connections and networking may lead to particularism and clientelism. This is difficult to distinguish from authoritarianism when it comes to the potential for abuse of power.

Extraconstitutional action should more properly be understood as not just overriding constraint but as overriding democracy itself. Such extraconstitutional action does not just "get the job done" but, in fact, deprives the people of democratic power. To deprive people of freedom of speech does not just serve to eliminate meddlesome critics and achieve order but may, in fact, disempower the people. Constitutionalists should seek to engender discourse and empowerment. The institutions of constitutional government are enfranchising in nature; if functioning well they may work to engage the citizens in a political conversation about popular concerns and values. In a modern complex society this is often the venue for values and development discourse. If constitutionalism is openly accepted as the venue for political choice rather than merely constraint, then the ensuing discourse in this venue may create respect for its important constraints and processes. To better understand this claim we must consider the constitutive process.

It is in the constitutive process that constitutionalism's discourse engendering and empowering roles come to fruition. This can be considered at two levels: the constitution-making process and constitutional implementation. Constitution making is where the explicit constitutional conversation usually begins. A constitutional assembly is a powerful venue for discourse about basic political values; this is especially true because such assemblies usually are called on the heels of a national crisis, which is inherently engaging. In recent decades the East

Asian landscape has been riddled with constitution-making exercises. The 1980s and 1990s constitution writing in the Philippines and Hong Kong offer prominent, seemingly successful examples. In describing the constitution-making process Jon Elster describes a venue where passion, interest, and reason operate. There are both upstream and downstream constraints, as well as processes for consensus building and broadening bases of support. Upstream constraints consider political settlements and may also protect members of the former regime. For the Hong Kong Basic Law, as with the postwar Japanese constitution, the upstream constraints were all but overwhelming. Downstream constraints look to ratification or acceptance. In the Philippines, after the people-power revolution, downstream acceptance was the substantial constraint.

After the founding of a constitution, successful implementation of constitutional government depends on appreciation of the discursive architecture in the ongoing processes of governance. More commonly appreciated here are the institutions for checks and balances. These include institutions to control purse strings in regimes ranging from medieval estates to modern parliaments, and veto and administrative control in the modern executive. At present, nearly every constitutional government in East Asia manifests some elements of this.

Less commonly understood is the positive discursive machinery of constitutional judicial review, the power whereby courts review laws enacted by the elected branches of government for conformity to the constitution. In both Asia and the West, this judicial role has sometimes been attacked as an affront to efficient and effective government, and sometimes as an affront to democracy. One should be suspicious of the efficiency-based motives of such attacks. In developed constitutional systems, constitutional judicial review has become the premier institution for securing human rights. More important, constitutional judicial review may also serve as the engine for the basic constitutional conversation about political values and commitments. This constitutional conversation proceeds as legislatures pass laws, courts respond, and legislatures pass new laws. Even though much of East Asia has adopted Western civil and common law legal systems, only a few countries have fully functioning systems of constitutional judicial rcview. At present Japan, the Philippines, and Hong Kong are prominent examples of where this power is vested in the ordinary courts, as is more commonly done in common law systems. A civil law style of constitutional court has existed in Taiwan for decades but has only recently, with the termination of martial law, begun to function effectively. South Korea has also instituted such a centralized constitutional court. For the authoritarian regimes of the region, both historically and at present, little or no judicial constraint is the norm. Even where the power of constitutional judicial review formally exists, in an authoritarian environment it is unlikely that judges can be counted on to assertively carry out such a role. Under such circumstances, the positive discourse-engendering role argued for here is out of the question.

Constitutional theorists recognize, however, that when issues of fundamental constitutional concern arise in established democratic systems, constitutional judicial review of legislation is not the sole discursive engine for crafting state-based solutions to broader societal concerns. At moments of crisis, what Stephen Krasner calls punctuated equilibrium, the entire people may be mobilized to civic action or intense reflection on political value concerns of fundamental importance. In normal times, the people may be content with representation and constitutional judicial review while they largely focus on private affairs; at times of what Bruce Ackerman calls constitutional politics the level of civic action may become extraordinary. Ackerman identifies three "republics" in U. S. history, before and after the Civil

War and in the modern regulatory social welfare state initiated in the 1930s by the New Deal. There is evidence of such mobilization and fundamental change in the recent South Korean and Japanese constitutional politics of reform and resistance to corruption. Considerable civic action and a fundamental change in political attitude also accompanied the post-1987 constitutional reforms in Taiwan. The recent overthrow of Suharto in Indonesia signals a major constitutional change of this civically engaging variety, and perhaps eventually a new constitution-making process.

Indigenization of Constitutionalism

With a firm commitment to the constitutional fundamentals in place, a premier concern is that constitutionalism plant its roots firmly in the local soil. Aung Sang Suu Kyi argues that as long as there is a genuine commitment to modern democratic values there is room for variation in local institutional embodiment. It is through local institutional embodiment (indigenization) that constitutionalism more directly responds to the above-cited concerns with values and development. Indigenization affords an appropriate response to cultural relativist and developmentalist concerns. For indigenous institutions to work, however, the constitutional fundamentals of democracy, that is, human rights and the rule of law, must be in place. Otherwise, under modern authoritarianism, the local community may be left with an implanted hegemonic discourse constructive of authoritarian power and destructive of genuine community values. Local institutional embodiment may include traditional organizations and practices and more contemporary institutions responsive to developmental concerns. Below, I consider the ways in which constitutional structures respond to both the cultural concerns raised in the Asian values debate and to developmental concerns likely to arise in post authoritarian constitutional democracies.

Constitutionalism and political culture – If a fundamental aim of constitutionalism is to engender political discourse, then constitutionalists should consider the ways in which local culture and traditions may facilitate such discourse, under the umbrella of the core constitutional commitments discussed above. It is in local institutional embodiment that substantive communitarian concerns can be addressed. As with the constitutional fundamentals, the notions of representation and the rule of law afford useful categories for analysis. Local grassroots and minority representation may be achieved through contemporary institutions that secure autonomy or minority rights, or through recognition of traditional ethnic or religious groups. The aim is for a realistic discourse that is anchored in the community but responsive to the contemporary urban and industrial or postindustrial conditions where increasing numbers of us live.

Locally sensitive representation may include attention to the usual geographic political institutional options, such as federalism or autonomy, which allow for local governance in a large national system. It may also include consideration of various electoral models that seem likely to increase representation of diverse groups and minority interests. Other forms of representation may include substantive or symbolic recognition of distinct ethnic, religious, or linguistic communities in which traditional leaders assume leadership roles. This may be achieved in various ways. It may include, for example, a continuing role, symbolic or substantive, for traditional monarchs, such as is evident in contemporary Malaysia, Japan, and Thailand. Special minority group rights may be combined with individual rights; in East Asia there are many traditional indigenous groups that are afforded varied degrees of recognition in the local constitutional system.

This experience of multicultural concerns is not unique to East Asia, encouraging consideration of practices elsewhere. Arend Lijphart has described the effort by elites to overcome the destabilizing effect of cultural fragmentation in Europe as consociational democracy. It is noteworthy that Lijphart employs the term democracy. A bargain across cleavage lines that only includes the elite strata would be merely authoritarian oligarchy and not likely secure a channel for constructing popular will. The use of various forms of local institutional embodiment, along with core constitutional commitments, may engender more confidence in the system, encourage local connectedness to the constitutional order, and facilitate genuine values discourse.

Legal structures may also address important indigenous concerns. This may include, for example, allowing for the application of religious or tribal laws. Here democratic commitments and basic rights must be emphasized. Traditional values can be renovated in a public values discourse that sustains important indigenous concerns while maintaining core constitutional commitments. Several possibilities may be considered. In societies with long traditions of citizen petition of leaders, a mechanism for petitioning elected officials could be employed or, perhaps, a modern version thereof, the ombudsman. Even a traditional monarch, who may retain symbolic and ceremonial functions, may take on an ombudsman-like role in a post monarchical democratic society. Such tradition-bound institutions may open better avenues of communication. Even when contemporary institutions are employed, in practice they may be expected to take on indigenous characteristics. Contemporary institutions such as human rights tribunals, election commissions, or corruption-fighting bodies may be employed to address those contemporary problems that neither the core constitutional nor traditional institutions adequately respond to. The goal in all cases is orderly processes of discursive engagement or empowerment.

Hegemonic claims of adherence to Asian values without a commitment to the core constitutional fundamentals are unlikely to engender a healthy values discourse or contribute to long-term public trust. In this regard one might contrast the constitutional paths of modern Japan and China. While these countries bear comparison due to similar traditional values and similar encounters with the modern West, the end result has produced striking differences, in many ways explainable by their contrasting postwar constitutional paths. Postwar Japan has taken a liberal constitutional path, but there has been substantial indigenization in practice. Yet, with the fundamentals in place, the constitution does seem to work to encourage a core discussion on fundamental political commitments. Indigenization even encompasses its formal practice of constitutional judicial review; though the courts are noted for taking a conservative posture, often offering only constitutional guidance, they have still played an active role in key constitutional issues. This system has afforded increased rights protection and does seem to take constitutionalism seriously. Elsewhere in the system, even the process of reform in respect to one-party dominance has proceeded in an orderly fashion and has engendered renewed public concern with corruption and enforcement of legal norms.

China, on the other hand, has rejected a commitment to the liberal constitutional fundamentals. China's public discourse has tended to advance a hegemonic view concerning the constitutional fundamentals of democracy, human rights and the rule of law, that people challenge at their peril. Constitutional judicial review is not provided, the constitution allowing instead, at least in theory, for a top-down legislative supervision by people's congresses (at the center the National People's Congress, or NPC), which are themselves not subject to competitive elections and are dominated from the center. If review occurs at all it is either through informal guidance or through the passage of laws. A collectivist notion of rights subjects the rights of the individual to the interests of the state. The public order situation is a conflict-laden one in which the Public Security Bureau and the military must play a central role. While engaging in economic reform, the regime has engendered increased diversification of interests (implicating both values and developmental concerns) for which inadequate representation is secured. Commitment to legality, under the theory of rule by law, is shaky at best, encouraging increased corruption as the economic reform process goes forward. This has produced a values vacuum that society is hard put to deal with. There is growing evidence of a concern in opening up democratic and legal channels for representation of diverse interests. Under the current authoritarian, top-down, unitary state such representation is virtually nonexistent, and corruption is the only effective channel available. Opening up appropriate legal and democratic channels will not automatically solve the current problems, but such a move may offer hope for crafting orderly solutions in the future.

Local institutional embodiment and economic development – Many of the same indigenization arguments addressed in relation to cultural values in the preceding have obvious connection, as well, to economic developmental concerns. Recognition of distinct cultural groups clearly has market and developmental implications: such groups address their distinct developmental problems and attract investment in various resources. Beyond multicultural concerns, however, economic concerns implicate a wide range of local constitutional issues. I find it useful to group these general issues around three categories where it can be seen that authoritarian practices fundamentally shape the post authoritarian order, including neutral borrowing, reacting against the authoritarian order, and copying authoritarian practices. It should be remembered that this concern with economic interest is a very old component in the constitutional equation, having manifested itself profoundly in the earliest written constitutional experiments in the United States in such things as, for example, federalism and the commerce power. I highlight only a few examples from East Asia where people as the economic actors have fundamentally shaped the constitutional order in response to local concerns.

The category of neutral borrowing refers to the attempt to simply identify or adapt a constitutional structure from outside the system to complete or fill out the constitutional order without a severe reactive component. In such contexts, constitutionalists are essentially looking for the best idea to secure the order required for the system to operate. The Japanese constitution includes components that fit this notion. It is true that the constitution as a whole and certain of its provisions (e.g., the peace provisions) were put in place by the Allied occupation authorities and postwar Japanese people as a reaction against previous excesses. But many of the institutional components imposed by the outside drafters were viewed rather neutrally by the Japanese people, who had to interpret or apply them. From such a perspective this constitution was an imported document. The institution of constitutional judicial review is a case in point. As noted above, through a very Japanese process of interpretation and implementation this institution underwent an indigenization process, incorporating a conservative judicial guidance role akin to the Japanese developmental practice of "administrative guidance." In spite of their passive posture, the courts have played a pivotal role in economic issues ranging from pollution to corruption. Over time, judicial review has become a very indigenous instrument for addressing fundamental constitutional concerns.

The second category is for post authoritarian democratic forces to react in a negative way against certain authoritarian practices. The peace provision of the Japanese constitution, which seeks to limit use of military force to defense, is just one prominent example in East Asia. Political provisions limiting the president to one term in both South Korea and the Philippines are other obvious examples of reaction to authoritarian excesses of prolonged dictatorship and corruption. There are more profound ways that authoritarian order shapes postauthoritarian practices in reactive ways. Jang Jip Choi describes an authoritarian South Korea that employed a rather harsh form of export-led developmentalism, with a heavy emphasis on the national interest. This produced three essentially reactive cleavages in the politics of the authoritarian period, over the issues of democracy versus dictatorship, distribution versus developmentalism, and reunification. The first of these produced the middle class–led democratic transformation and a firm reaction against indirect election of the president when this idea was proposed. The second cleavage imported a strong concern with equality and social justice into transition politics. Concern with worker protections relating to labor organizing, job security and welfare have become fundamental concerns shaping postauthoritarian South Korea. Choi emphasizes the importance of institutional mechanisms through which workers can articulate their views. In the most recent economic crisis, the political leadership is confronted with the need to move against the authoritarian cronyism of the large South Korean companies, while not being seen to have been insensitive to worker interests. The third cleavage of reunification or not has been a central theme of opposition forces and has imposed a heavy national security component on the political system. Overall, the postauthoritarian system can be seen to have been fundamentally shaped, in ways with profound implications for the developmental order, by reaction against authoritarian excesses and the problems of a divided Korean peninsula.

When it comes to the third category, in copying the perceived developmental successes of the authoritarian period many of the same examples are illustrative. As the economic crisis of the late 1990s reveals, many of the institutional arrangements of authoritarian developmentalism were left in place by the postauthoritarian democratic regimes. Given the perceived successes of the East Asian "economic miracles," this is not a surprise. Democratic governments throughout the region have felt compelled to leave in place the systems of bureaucratic control that were pervasive under these seemingly successful developmental models. The prevalent attitude was that "if it ain't broke don't fix it." For this reason, many of the democratic governments of the region have continued to be plagued by problems of bureaucratic corruption and cronyism that were often endemic to the authoritarian developmental model. Especially after the economic crisis that began in 1997 a shift to a reactive position may now creep into economic institutions, such as reinforced systems of central bank control and corruption-fighting institutions. But, to date, the bureaucratic structures of authoritarian developmentalism have continued to flourish in some postauthoritarian governments. The South Korean example discussed above (which is now the subject of a reactive response due to the economic crisis) is a case in point. Japanese developmental bureaucracies have until recently likewise remained in place, even as political reform proceeds.

The phenomenon of copying the more questionable authoritarian economic practices, noted immediately above, does not exhaust the possibilities. In Hong Kong, the prudent fiscal policies of the colonial period have been written into the postauthoritarian Basic Law. The prudence of these policies is yet to be tested. One might expect a lot of the decentralizing policies of the current authoritarian Chinese government in setting up autonomous regions and economic zones to shape a federal China in a postauthoritarian future. If this occurred, it would constitute a hybrid of reaction against excessive central control and a copying of liberalizing decentralizing tendencies. In either case, in East Asia authoritarian practices have had a pervasive effect on postauthoritarian order in ways that especially address or affect developmental concerns or policies.

Summary

The choice of authoritarianism; second, that under East Asia's current condition of substantial economic development an authoritarian regime can no longer adequately respond to diverse developmental concerns; third, there is the positive role of constitutionalism in constructing empowering conversations in modern democratic development and as a venue for values and developmental discourse; and fourth, there is the salient importance, especially in cross-cultural and developmental contexts, of indigenization of constitutionalism through local institutional embodiment. It is the linkage of these points that connects the constitutional regime of a given state or similar territorial community to the international processes of human rights and establishes the importance of domestic human rights practices.

At the dawn of the twenty-first century, in a world that is increasingly fragmented and integrated at the same time, the concept of the state has begun to take on a new meaning. A certain level of fragmentation has meant that there are more territorial communities than ever before that claim state status, while other non state territorial communities have arisen whose importance matches that of states. This fragmentation has meant that local institutions of self-rule are very important in the discursive processes of constructing local values and responding to local developmental needs. In modern urban industrial and post-industrial societies, the institutions of constitutional government and human rights have become increasingly important in this constructive process. These institutions construct local order and are constructive of the diverse entities that make up the international state system.

8

Protesting Rights of Foreign Migrant in Asia

Introduction

The case of foreign migrant workers in Asia presents an opportunity for examining two elements intrinsic to the debate over human rights and Asian values. First, it allows us to focus on a group of individuals who are not counted as members of the national society. Whereas the host government will be clear about its responsibilities towards its own nationals, that responsibility may not carry over to non-members. Instead, migrants may be rated as outsiders, without clear minimum standards of humane treatment. They may even find themselves actively unwanted by the host society. What is of particular concern to us, however, is how the debate over standards for migrant workers has evolved, since it sets in relief local approaches to the humane treatment of a group of people held as distinct from the ordinary members of society.

Second, their case provides a context for examining the political processes whereby new shared understandings of humane treatment are being established understandings usually seen to integrate local frameworks with aspects of international human rights. A particularly salient question is whether these processes might lead to setting regional standards for humane treatment, without appeal to rights as such.

Two alternative types of political process have contributed to clarifying and expanding the standards for treatment of migrants in individual Asian states. States that support civil and political liberties for their own nationals provide a distinctive context for publicly negotiating over the status of foreign migrants with regard to rights and protective standards. In contrast, in states that restrict freedoms of association or expression for the sake of the general good, few indigenous supports exist to encourage improved treatment of foreign migrants, let alone clarification of their rights. Instead, the sending foreign governments, subject to their own internal political forces, may choose to pressure the receiving country to make improvements. Without a strong commitment to rights, the receiving government confronts needing to find elements in its own political or legal system on which to base such alterations.

The two types share in common a net result of increased protections for foreign migrants, but not to the same degree. In the former case, the motivations for expanded protections have included explicit concerns about rights expressed within a domestic political process; in the latter, much of the motivation has stemmed from considerations of foreign relations. While in the former case a universalistic approach to human rights has driven policy change, the latter case has involved a search for an 'overlapping consensus' over norms of humane treatment that would span the divergent positions of the participants.

Foreign migrant workers in Asia have entered contemporary public debate in conjunction with their heightened visibility. Between 1990 and 1994 alone, approximately 8.5 million migrant labourers from Asia were deployed abroad; of the 2 million who migrated in 1994, approximately 25 per cent went to other countries within Asia. Some workers have migrated from South-east Asia to industrialized North-east Asia; some within South-east Asia; some within the East Asian region; and others increasingly from South Asia to South-east and East Asia. In migrating to take jobs as marginally skilled workers (whatever their educational qualifications), they may do so through formal short-term contract schemes or training arrangements, or they may choose 'clandestine' or 'illegal' employment.

Governments on the receiving side, desiring to maintain a supply of labour for their thriving miracle economies, developed policy mechanisms to manage this migration mechanisms that would further shape some of the problems that migrants would confront. Taiwan initiated in 1989 a system to import foreign contract labour for limited stays. In 1991, South Korea established a system for foreigners' industrial training, and in 1993, it began to systematically set quotas for importing foreign trainees to meet labour demand. Singapore, while having employed migrant labour as a means of meeting labour demand for some time, tightened its controls over temporary migration in 1989. Hong Kong initiated schemes for importing contract labour in 1989. Japan remained an exception in that, despite business group pressures in the late 1980s, immigration control revisions (1990) allowed admission of only migrants of Japanese ancestry as foreign unskilled labour. More recently, Thailand instituted in 1996 a system for registering migrants already in the country illegally, and Malaysia began more stringent enforcement of its regulations in 1997 after a period of registering undocumented workers. In these countries, the systems established introduced a layer of administrative management that simultaneously eased and restricted the entry of foreign migrants to provide labour that would support favourable growth rates.

By late 1997, several countries were both importers and exporters of labour, and certain economies in the region had become dependent on foreign labour. In South-east Asia, the Malaysian government estimate commonly quoted in news coverage in late 1997 and early 1998 was 2 million foreign workers, of which 1.2 million had work permits, in a total population of 21 million. In Thailand, newspaper coverage in early 1998 referred to general estimates of approximately 1 million or more foreign workers in a workforce of about 33 million. In November 1997, Singapore relied on over 450,000 low- or medium-skilled non-Singaporeans for 26 per cent of its labour force. As of October 1997, Taiwan had 254,000 documented foreign workers, or approximately 3 per cent of the labour force, and South Korea had an estimated 234,000 foreign workers.

Government measures toward foreign labour after the onset of economic crisis in late 1997 kept shifting. As governments confronted rising unemployment among their own nationals, they either continued with policing efforts toward foreign workers that were already underway, cancelled immediate plans for admitting foreign workers, redeployed foreign workers to other sectors of their economies, initiated new programmes to expel undocumented workers, or took some combination of these actions. The Thai government had announced a plan to expel all of its estimated 800,000 undocumented migrants, mostly from Myanmar, by 1 May 1998, and by 31 August had deported approximately 261,000. In South Korea, about 20,000 foreign workers exited in January and February 1998, after the government gave undocumented foreign workers a grace period to leave without penalties, but by early 1999, newspaper reports indicated that industrial trainees and other foreign workers were once again entering the country. Malaysia, which had also been in the process of a heightened policing campaign before the economic downturn, continued to rely on foreign workers throughout. Despite its stated intention not to renew permits of workers already there, by October 1998 the government had approved the admission of 190,000 foreign workers to meet demand in construction, plantation, and manufacturing. Likewise, though the large numbers of Indonesians fleeing to Malaysia in early 1998 had led to overcrowded detention camps and deportations reported widely in the media, by November, the Malaysian government had announced that it would rely on Indonesia to provide the large majority of 220,000 foreign workers to be admitted in 1999.

Until late 1997, however, several Asian governments had been attempting steadily to improve their systems for managing migration and for monitoring compliance with regulations. Among the problems to which they were responding were contradictions in policy mechanisms, failures in the system of social supports, and substandard employment conditions. The examples of discussion and policy change prior to the onset of crisis furnish a perspective on Asian governments' recognition of these outsiders as deserving of equal protections and illustrate the challenges for negotiating regional standards across widely differing political and economic systems.

Foreign Migrants in Asia and Human Rights

The visible social presence of foreign migrant workers in several Asian countries leads the respective governments to make choices with serious implications for human rights. A transparent motivation for some of these governments is to limit migrants' terms of stay to prevent settlement and to restrict workers' social position to one of a productive resource. Even so, with increased numbers of migrants abroad, the incidence of abuse, deception, criminal victimization, exploitative wages, and other forms of worker mistreatment has drawn attention to the inadequacies of regulatory measures. As a consequence, the debate that has occurred among academics, non-governmental organizations, and government officials has extended beyond migration control mechanisms to include the substance of rights and protections for migrants. While similar issues have also challenged North American and European states, the discussion in Asian states remains contingent upon different political and institutional contexts, with consequences for foreign migrants as to whether and how protections may be secured and enhanced.

The primary substantive issues for discussion here are integral to migrants' experience and pose problems for many of them: their basic protections *vis-à-vis* employers and, in conjunction with that, the impact of documentation status on workers' access to protections. Such protections, however, remain situated within a broader set of stipulations specific to foreign migrants such as whether documented migrants are permitted to join labour unions or the extent of labour standards applied to them by the host country and a still broader context of the rights and freedoms extended to nationals of the host country.

In Asian states, much as in European or North American states, a hierarchy of rights for non-nationals governs, yet this hierarchy is bounded by the local system of rights for nationals. It is not uncommon for access to protections to vary according to immigration status ranging from citizen to permanent resident alien to documented migrant to undocumented worker. In industrialized democratic states, foreign migrant labourers, while unlikely to possess political rights, generally possess civil rights of association, expression, and access to the courts, although these may be somewhat constrained. They often possess economic and social rights in the form of labour and social protections similar to those of local workers; they are dependent upon whatever the policy regime in place is. Undocumented workers, lacking legal residence, have the fewest rights, and are subject to likely further consequences of exploitation by employers and a *de facto* loss of the few rights they may technically enjoy in some systems. These distinctions in immigration categories may entail corollary differences in access to rights and protections in Asian countries as well, but the substantive effect varies. The rights and protections accorded to nationals of the host countries constitute a base that is uneven across Asian countries, and this has consequences for the ability of migrants, and nationals sympathetic to them, to associate freely, to pursue officially sanctioned protections for foreign migrants, and to work to revise policy mechanisms.

The perceived fairness of documentation status as a determinant for migrants' access to many rights and protections is undermined often by failings in the system for managing migration. Migrants' freely-made individual choices may not be the reason for their undocumented status, a situation that introduces ambiguities into the discussion of the rights of migrants. Circumstances over which a migrant has little control, such as the behaviours of employers or recruiters and contradictions in policy mechanisms, may affect their status or their choice to relinquish documented status. For instance, when failures in implementation, monitoring, or policy design exist, undocumented status or fear of losing documented status may dissuade workers from seeking assistance when they are abused or exploited. Likewise, the potential penalties may deter nationals from working through the system to advocate on foreigners' behalf. For such reasons, the UN International Convention on the Rights of All Migrant Workers and Members of Their Families goes to lengths to specify extensive rights for 'undocumented' workers in recognition of their special vulnerability to exploitation, but it also maintains a distinction between documented and undocumented workers and their rights.

State mechanisms for regulating migration, alongwith their implementation, have a huge bearing on whether or not a worker obtains and maintains legal residence. This may occur because standards specified are so uncoordinated with market conditions and living standards that they are exploitative. In South Korea, officials had recognized by 1995 that the minimal compensation and conditions sustained through the officially-sanctioned trainee programme were encouraging 'runaways' to choose better-paid but undocumented work; revising the system led to a subsequent reduction in those numbers.

A state may fail to monitor and implement adequately regulations concerning labour contracts, labour standards, or employer-provided housing and other benefits. For instance, if a government fails to monitor whether employers are living up to their contracts with migrants, or if a government's own border officials collaborate with traffickers of migrant workers, the workers will most likely be unable to obtain relief. To respond to the former type of problem, the Malaysian and Philippine governments have conducted talks to promote improved monitoring of a sort that might provide abused workers with an alternative to choosing between illegal work or returning home.

Criminal activity by employers and recruiters, left unmonitored, may similarly result in workers ending up unwittingly without documentation and deprived of a basis for seeking relief from abusive conditions. In some of the personal accounts of migrants circulated by non-governmental organizations in Japan, Taiwan, and elsewhere, workers have believed that they were complying with regulations to obtain proper documentation and legal employment, when in fact they have been deceived and manipulated by illicit recruiters or employers. In such cases, particularly if the employer holds the passport of the worker (a frequent occurrence throughout Asia), fleeing an abusive and criminal employer often means abandoning one's proof of identity and living fully underground. To respond to criminal exploitation of female entertainers, the Japanese and Philippine governments have conducted regular discussions since 1988, and each has incrementally introduced changes in practices.

Accompanying these problems, a second set of questions related to human rights affects prospects for revisions to solve them satisfactorily. What types of conditions enable foreign migrants to pursue protections when policies are enforced ineffectively? Similarly, what types of conditions promote improvements in policy to make it easier and more rational for migrants to maintain a documented status and to expand the protections available to legal migrants? Clearly, other actors besides the migrants play a role in the host government's choice to enhance protections for migrants, whether they are non-governmental organizations that support migrants, domestic interest groups, or foreign governments concerned about the welfare of their own nationals overseas. But which actors, through what means, become pivotal depends on features of the political system. General conditions of human freedoms both for nationals of the host country and for the migrants themselves determine what processes will be available for representing migrants' needs effectively.

For instance, in some of the examples mentioned in the preceding paragraphs, non-governmental organizations of the host country's nationals were instrumental in drawing attention to policy failures. Their familiarity with migrants' needs, which was a result of their support activities, prompted their advocacy on behalf of migrants. For these organizations to play such a role has required a context in which they have the freedom to associate and provide assistance, in which migrants have been able to seek assistance with impunity, and in which nationals have been able to gain access to government officials in their advocacy efforts.

Alternatively, in some cases, domestic interest groups, working on their own behalf, may end up calling for changes that benefit the migrants. For instance, in Thailand in 1996, objections by organized labour to legalizing foreign workers resulted in a government decision to apply the minimum wage to the foreigners (although the extent of enforcement is difficult to determine). Other generalized concerns for the social welfare may similarly stimulate provisions for health care and other benefits, as has been visible in Thai efforts to provide migrants with health care as a preventive public health measure. While the latter example did not necessarily require a context of civil and political freedoms, the former example depended upon conditions of open political debate.

Finally, officials of the sending governments have entered into discussion in a manner that has created further incentives for change. Foreign sending governments most notably the Philippines have taken government-to-government initiatives in response to their own domestic pressures over the issue and as a response to the chronic problems of their nationals overseas. Likewise, the Philippine government has increased the support services that it provides to its overseas contract workers. While the government-to-government process may not depend on a context of human rights to have an impact, civil and political freedoms in the sending country are significant for putting pressure on the government to make migrants' needs an issue in their foreign relations.

In sum, alternative processes afford means through which foreign workers' needs can gain a constructive response. State and societal participants work within the existing framework of the legal system, workers' protective measures, enforcement institutions, and rules regarding freedom of speech, association, and political participation. But when such a framework constrains rights of society's members, let alone migrants, the opportunities for change through domestic processes to benefit foreign workers are limited.

Contrasting Cases of Human Rights

Two contrasting cases highlight the manner in which the different priorities given to rights influence alternatives for improving the conditions of migrant workers by receiving countries. When a host government maintains a relatively open civil society in which non governmental organizations and even foreign migrants can mobilize, policy adjustments and protections have been possible from within through governmental processes or through the courts even if assisted by bilateral government-to-government relationships. When the host government limits freedoms of expression and association within its own borders, improvements depend far more on the government-to government relationship; the dynamic of *that* relationship, however, may also depend indirectly on domestic political pressures and non governmental activism within the sending country.

For such reasons of process, the conditions that affect the quality of migrants' lives extend well beyond mechanisms for managing migration or the protections they specify. Social, legal, and political contexts interact with specific policy provisions to shape the sum total of conditions that migrants face. They may offer resources for advocacy, further policy change, and clarification of rights; or they may function to restrict the alternatives to which migrants have resort in the event of abuse or violations of contract, thus elevating the importance of government-to-government relations as an alternative medium. These contexts provide more than just a vehicle for discussion. As the South Korean and Singaporean examples illustrate, they offer conceptual justifications and institutional resources on which to ground protections for foreign temporary workers.

South Korea

Although the economic crisis that began in fall 1997 triggered a temporary lull in South Korean demand for unskilled foreign workers as industrial trainees, the tenor of discussion has continued to be one of improving the system in a manner that ensures protections for these workers. Many political participants' recognition of contradictions in the system and the need to clarify the rights of industrial trainees as workers had already led to changes. Premised on a respect for the rights of workers, this debate incorporated a visible role for industrial interests, activism by non-governmental organizations, and governmental efforts to eliminate policy contradictions and failures.

The system for relying on foreign workers expanded steadily over the 1990s. In 1991, South Korea established its system for foreigners' industrial training, and in 1993, it began systematically to set quotas for importing 'trainees'. At the end of 1996, there were over 210,000 foreign workers in South Korea, of whom about 70,000 were industrial trainees and approximately 130,000 were classified as 'illegal' (meaning that they had either entered illegally, had deserted their positions as industrial trainees for other better-paid work, or were working in violation of another visa status). By October 1997, the estimated number of foreigners working in South Korea was about 234,000.

Over the first two-thirds of the 1990s, the inadequacies of this system drew attention from non-governmental organizations and government agencies alike. The system failed to protect clearly the rights of these trainees, and inherent policy contradictions made it rational for trainees to desert for 'illegal' work. 'Trainees', because they lacked the employment status of 'worker', were not protected by minimum labour standards, despite their legal immigration status. Even so, the South Korean political system gave both South Korean non-governmental organizations and trainees themselves adequate freedom of speech and association to champion reforms and to provide supports to foreign workers, documented or not. Organizations such as the Korea Research Institute for Workers' Human Rights and Justice and the Association for Foreign Workers'

Human Rights have provided an umbrella for the many smaller organizations that support foreign migrants. In addition, some trainees organized, and protests by Nepalese trainees in January 1995 resulted in Labour Ministry regulations that brought conditions of trainees in line with those of workers. As a result, trainees obtained some benefits equivalent to those legislated for Korean workers, in the form of injury compensation, medical insurance, and so forth.

Even in the sluggish economic conditions of early 1997, the South Korean government and societal groups continued to discuss the rights of industrial trainees and the conditions of their stay, so as to revise this system of admitting foreign low-skilled workers. In September 1997, the government announced its plan that, as of 1 January 1998, workers who had fulfilled the two-year period of industrial traineeship were to become eligible for employment permits and for all of the rights that South Korean workers possess including the right to organize, to bargain collectively, and to strike. But conditions declined precipitously, and the South Korean government soon announced a moratorium on admitting industrial trainees for 1998 and subsequently issued directives to ensure that undocumented workers would leave. By summer 1999, however, demand for foreign workers and the estimates of those in the country illegally had both risen.

In the above South Korean discussion of policy revisions, concerns about rights were intertwined with an awareness that the policy as implemented was encouraging industrial trainees to defect and to choose undocumented labour. Initially, trainees received substantially lower compensation than Koreans doing the same work, and they were readily able to find much more remunerative work by leaving their trainee posts. Improving the level of trainee compensation had an impact by diminishing the incentives to leave for undocumented, but better-paying, employment: the 'runaway rate' declined steadily from 1994 through 1997.

By late 1997, coverage in the Korean English language press of the anticipated 1998 changes indicated that non Koreans would likely achieve parity with Koreans in wages and benefits as a result.

Such discussion of policy change soon was supplanted by that of dealing with widespread unemployment. By the beginning of 1999, however, the admission of industrial trainees had resumed and by mid 1999, requests by small- and medium-sized businesses for them had increased, despite domestic unemployment rates of 6.4 per cent as of July 1999.

Despite the instabilities, the South Korean case remains important for illustrating a process of extending and defining the rights of foreign migrant workers. That process has occurred in a context of political freedoms that allows nationals and foreigners to mobilize for change over policy inadequacies. The language of rights and the efforts to define workers' status so as to ensure rights has been at the heart of this incremental process of inclusion and change.

Singapore

In contrast to South Korea with its explicit embrace of rights, ideologically and institutionally Singapore presents a different set of resources for improving the standards of treatment for foreign migrants. Instead of domestic pressures and activism, government-to-government relations have been the main impetus for protections. The Singaporean government, for its part, has focused on enforcement of existing Singaporean law in a manner that responds to some of the complaints, and the mass media have co-operated by publicizing this stand. In the government's effort to satisfy external pressures, the legal system has become the institutional sphere of overlap between differing positions on rights.

Certainly, the dominant ideology minimizes the likelihood that government or Singaporean citizens would be vocal about protecting foreign migrants, at least with a rhetoric of rights. Even use of a rhetoric of the state's responsibility for the social and economic welfare of its citizens is unlikely, because such responsibility does not extend to non citizens. Furthermore, the ideology of responsibility to the collectivity, as Chua suggests, inhibits sensitivity to issues of individual rights for its members; this may make it doubly difficult to recognize or raise questions over humane treatment for outsiders. Government's stress on ideological consensus and its strategies for managing critical opinion foster 'a sense that participation must be conducted within the agenda and concepts generated and approved by the government itself'. These factors, supported by the implicit discouragements of an Internal Security Act, serve as deterrents to public discussion or advocacy that is not sanctioned by government.

That said, Singapore's reliance on foreign migrant labour occurs in a technocratic process of labour market management in which the state has the capacity to gain employers' compliance with its regulations. Singapore relies on low- or medium-skilled non-Singaporean labour for over 25 per cent of the work force. A system of work permits and levies is designed to satisfy but moderate demand for foreign labour. 'Work permits' are required for low-skilled and medium-skilled jobs, and employment passes for highly-skilled employees. Levies imposed on employers are intended to allow but constrain employment of foreign workers; dependency ceilings, which vary by sector, limit individual employers as to the proportion of foreigners they may hire.

Officials adjust the levies and dependency ceilings as conditions change: recent changes that reflect the Singaporean government's increased priority on moderately-skilled workers are one such example. In September 1997, the government announced new plans to yet further encourage the entry of 'foreign talent', particularly 'mid-level' skilled workers in jobs such as bus driver, equipment operator, technician, nurse, or teacher. Subsequent changes in levies announced in November 1997 included an increase in the levy for unskilled workers but decreases in the levy for skilled foreign workers.

This system is focused on smooth management of the labour market and foreign labour use, with little emphasis on worker protection. All the same, it suggests the extent of control that the state can exercise over employers and its readiness to impose sanctions on them when so motivated. In the mid-to-late 1990s, government efforts to enforce the system for employing foreign migrants increasingly focused on employers as the culpable parties when violations were uncovered. The government focused on prosecuting employers for violations concerning levies, dependency ceilings, work permits, and use of employees in jobs for which employers did not have authorization. While technically the workers found working illegally were also liable to arrest and penalties, media coverage sent a clear message that employers would be prosecuted.

In contrast with this administrative control of the labour market, the main impetus for protecting migrant workers has come from the country's foreign relations. In the absence of formal bilateral agreements, which the Singaporean government has consistently resisted, governments such as the Philippines and Indonesia have used sensational incidents that threaten Singapore's international image as occasions for urging consideration of the general conditions for their workers. The 1995 hanging of a Filipina maid for murder in Singapore triggered major debate within the Philippines over humane treatment of Filipinas abroad and resulted in a temporary downgrading of diplomatic relations between the two countries. In conjunction with restoring diplomatic relations and removing a ban against Filipina maids going to Singapore, the Philippine government significantly reorganized its overseas system of supports available to migrant workers. It has also imposed a minimum standard contract on recruiters from Singapore and it has refused licensing to certain recruiters.

Likewise, the Indonesian government called public attention to the treatment of their maids in Singapore in mid-1997. After a hideous case of abuse of a fifteen-year-old maid became a media topic over the summer of 1997, the Indonesian government called for a ban on maids going to Singapore until they could undergo preparatory orientations for coping with their overseas situations.

These diplomatic episodes with Association of South-east Asian Nation (ASEAN) allies account for the formulation of a protective solution compatible with Singaporean ideology. The Singaporean government has stressed enforcement of existing laws to prevent the physical abuse of foreign workers by employers. Media attention has stressed the penalties to be applied for molestation and other violent crimes, and it incorporates a paternalistic approach of educating employers about their liability. The Singapore Ministry of Labour, in response to the temporary ban on maids to Singapore by Indonesia, included the following as part of a press statement on 24 September 1997:

> *The Ministry takes a serious view of employers who ill-treat or abuse their foreign domestic workers. The Singapore government will act swiftly against errant employers guilty of ill-treating their workers. In addition to the penalties meted out under the law, errant employers and their spouses are permanently barred from future employment of foreign domestic workers.*

In taking this position, the government has focused on the issue of physical abuse and violence as it is proscribed by Singaporean law; it has not reversed its basic position of non-intervention regarding the employment contract. Instead, the shared condemnation of physical abuse and commitment to legal institutions constitutes the basis for an overlapping position between Singapore and the foreign governments involved. The motivation to co-operate with allies and to preserve international image, buttressed by customary pressures from the ASEAN relationship to resolve bilateral tensions, has resulted in a Singaporean response of stronger attention to enforcement of existing laws. Otherwise, the sending governments have found they must regulate behaviours through the recruiting system on their end to the possible extent.

Arguably, the sending governments were under similar pressures to express indignation and to speak out for migrants when these events occurred, to respond to public outcry at home and to mute criticism in the international press. Critics who speak for migrants may contend (as I have heard them do in conversation) that such actions amount to gestures without a commitment to their nationals abroad. Whether or not that is the case, the crucial question for the current discussion is whether the Singaporean government has changed anything in its handling of the mistreatment of migrants. The above evidence indicates that, in certain senses, it has.

Summary

The preceding discussion of South Korea and Singapore has presented two contrasting examples of processes that have resulted in incremental changes to protect foreign migrant workers by building on different assumptions and reasoning. In the case of South Korea, expansion of protections has depended on a domestic context of civil and political liberties, which has afforded opportunities for advocacy and change within the system. Beyond the process itself, argument and justifications have incorporated an explicit rhetoric of rights. By contrast, in Singapore, government-to-government relations have been the channel for change. To the extent that change has occurred, protections for foreign migrants have been built on stringent adherence to the legal system in applying penalties for violations of existing law. Rather than to assert the 'rights' of the migrants, the Singaporean government has asserted the 'wrongs' of employer abuse toward them. It has not changed the law, but has become attentive to its implementation so as to protect this group of outsiders whom society may perceive as not equally human or worthy of protections. Rather than rights, the normative basis for this inclusion has been the enforcement role of the state and a commitment to the legal system.

The two examples reaffirm that establishing principles for humane treatment whether in terms of rights or otherwise occurs within specific political processes and policy systems. Political institutions, legal institutions, and the particular rights enjoyed by nationals of the host country constitute significant factors that affect the treatment of migrants. Although these institutions may promote clarification of migrants' rights in some countries, in others the pressures from other governments are the main impetus for improving these workers' conditions. Whatever interests and identity the states of Asia may share, the divergence among them is such that finding a consensus over the status and treatment of migrants through political negotiation of regional norms remains a challenge.

What do these cases suggest about the potential for finding an overlap between concepts of basic universal rights and locally developed normative systems that evade a language of rights or that justify a position for rights that is contingent upon the good of the collectivity? In the one case, an explicit embrace of basic human rights for one's own nationals made it relatively easy to extend them to include this new group of foreign workers. But making the necessary concrete changes in policy additionally depended upon a context of civil and political liberties in which migrants could find assistance and citizens could advocate. In the second case, while the motivations and process available for exerting influence may have been mainly external, a compromise of sorts across ideological frameworks involved a more inclusive application of the law.

These patterns of adjustment suggest questions about the longer term likelihood that a accumulation of such solutions will eventuate in shared understandings and norms, if not fully accepted principles, of basic human rights across diverse political systems. Apprehensions, scepticism, and confusions will understandably accompany many readers' appraisal of whether it is possible to integrate a universalistic approach to human rights with other locally-specified approaches in a manner that will satisfy proponents of both views. Three issues that arise in the cases here warrant comment: the notion of 'human-ness'; potential scenarios involving government-to-government relations; and the difference between negotiated norms compared to a universalistic approach to human rights.

First, the notion of 'human-ness' as it indicates a universalistic basis for inclusion does not necessarily incorporate a stress on rights. The Singaporean attempt to apply more stringently its laws and regulations hinged upon a commitment to impersonal legal institutions, even though the motivation may have arisen from pressures in foreign relations. As a consequence, the government exercised a greater vigilance regarding enforcement to prevent 'wrongs' against foreign migrants, within existing laws, and to reinforce a notion of basic 'human-ness'. The obvious foreign relations motivation does not negate the implicit rationale which furnished a domestically acceptable justification for action by appealing to the legal system and the need to maintain it no matter who a victim or perpetrator might be. In other words, this response embodied an approach to the victims of abuse that was more socially inclusive and that, in effect, asserted migrants' equality as humans. Yet that response did not incorporate an affirmation of individual rights as such.

This expanded inclusiveness minus an affirmation of individual human rights, however, exhibits its limitations if one asks the means by which migrants who fall victim to abuse are to gain access to the legal system or how any substantive changes in the laws are to be made. Barring sanctioned efforts to change the law for citizens, the status quo of criminal law, employment law, and mechanisms for their monitoring will determine the extent of possible protections. For migrants to seek legal redress frequently requires some set of supports to encourage them or others to speak out and seek assistance; sometimes these are provided to a degree by the migrants' own governments. Yet migrants are unlikely to be able to pursue such assistance themselves and doing so could put them at further risk. In a social context in which the local members tend not to speak out (for whatever reasons), how this legal inclusiveness can have an impact bears watching.

Second, government-to-government interactions provide a set of processes through which attention to human needs and protections is strengthened, but the basis for this and the possible alternative scenarios need to be examined further. State-to-state relations may contribute positively to the welfare of foreign migrant workers, even to the limited extent described above, but this is by no means guaranteed. Within a generally co-operative bilateral relationship characterized by mutual economic or political dependence, reciprocity may serve as the basis for a sense of 'extended' societal membership among nationals of the two allies.

Arguably, for states with a fairly established history of bilateral collaboration and possibly co-operation in multilateral contexts, this familiarity may help to breed government and societal openness to a status of 'quasi-membership' for the foreign nationals of the counterpart state. This is not the same as creating a shared human identity, but it is part of a process of enlarging the umbrella of social acknowledgement for groups who may not be considered 'members', but worthy of equal treatment. Whatever agreements governments may negotiate over migrants, their effectiveness remains dependent on the sense of interconnectedness, perceived reciprocity, and shared interests between not just governments, but the members of the respective societies. Without this perceived interconnectedness, any historical tendencies to cast certain foreign nationals as an enemy, for political, cultural, or economic reasons, will persist. Whatever formal agreements states may negotiate, it is unlikely that there will be much societal will to live up to state directives, and the societal co-operation needed to enforce them will be lacking.

A co-operative relationship between governments, however, in no way guarantees improved conditions for workers, for reciprocity may work in more than one direction. If neither government plays the role of advocate on behalf of the migrants, the only potential incentives to improve conditions will be perceived economic or administrative effects. Instead, the governments may collaborate in policing without providing has helped to limit the likelihood of disagreements and inability to come to some common understandings, particularly given the political and economic divergences among countries and the disparities in their stands on human rights generally. Up to now, the norms of regional co-operation, which stress maintaining a 'comfort level' and relegating tenser issues to the bilateral context, have supported the bilateral approach and have fostered resistance to a regional consideration of the treatment of migrants in terms of human rights or criticizing another states' internal practices.

Recently, however, the push for an ASEAN initiative has heightened in response to issues that cannot be handled bilaterally, for instance third-country migrants, the policing of transnational trafficking rings, and the increasing incentives to migrate due to adverse conditions in certain countries of the region. In August 1998, the ASEAN Inter-Parliamentary Organization General Assembly issued a resolution on transnational labour migration with strong recommendations for actions by member states. As the initiation of an ASEAN Free Trade Area in 2003 approaches, the pressures for a collective approach to the handling of migration are likely to increase.

Although a multilateral discussion may be emerging, any discussion of standards for human protection will occur in conjunction with discussions on policing, human trafficking, public health, and other issues. Contributing to this discussion will be certain governments and numerous non-governmental organizations who have called for both a regional discussion of migration and the ratification of the United Nations International Convention on the Protection of Rights of All Migrant Workers and Members of Their Families. Host countries not only in Asia, but throughout the world, have resisted ratifying this convention, but the possibility remains that host countries might choose to participate in an Asian regional agreement could they be persuaded that such would benefit their individual economies or their ability to manage labour migration. Even if a set of minimum standards for the treatment of migrants were to be established through some regional multilateral forum, enforcement would likely depend on voluntary compliance as a product of the pressures that states brought to bear on one another.

The message to be taken from the above discussion is that there is potential for a communicative process eventually resulting in improved protections for foreign migrants. This, however, is unlikely to produce a set of regional norms equivalent to human rights principles. For improving basic protections for foreign migrants, the conditions of political, civil, and social rights of nationals of the host country will continue to be significant contextual factors, but state-to-state relations will provide a limited alternative avenue for improving protections for foreign workers when the domestic impetus is not there. Likewise, when the Asian countries move toward establishing a regional framework for managing migration, the protection of migrants will be one of many issues to be addressed.

9

Globalization's Impact on Human Rights

Introduction

Globalization is considered by many as *the* major development in world society, particularly since the removal of the Berlin Wall in 1989. Indeed, Thomas Friedman maintains that globalization is the central organizing principle of the post–Cold War world, an international order that has replaced the Cold War system. Yet the processes leading to the contemporary phenomenon date back centuries. Marco Polo played a major role in inaugurating worldwide commerce in the thirteenth and fourteenth centuries, which eventually led to a flourishing spice trade from the "Orient" to Europe. Subsequently mercantilism extracted precious metals from the Asian and American continents for the coffers of European monarchies, an extensive Mediterranean trade transported goods to Europe, Arab traders seeking to extend their commerce settled in East Africa, and the European-initiated African slave trade evolved in West Africa which, through its triangular structure, also incorporated into that system the territories of the Caribbean and the American colonies. The emergence of the world capitalist system during what Immanuel Wallerstein called "the long 16th century" had been preceded, as Janet Abu-Lughod documents, by a world system in the thirteenth and fourteenth centuries, centered in Asia. Even at its earliest beginnings, the globalized mercantile system had little concern for the human rights of individuals in those areas caught up in its trappings.

The rise of capitalism in Western European states during the nineteenth century, made possible by scientific advances and technological innovation, led to the development of imperialism and the establishment of colonial empires. The "second" imperialism of the late nineteenth century established binding political and economic links across the globe. Colonialism as a system of political rule by the industrialized Western states was accompanied by economic exploitation and the increasing dependence of the non-industrialized on the industrialized world. Traditional subsistence economies and their trade patterns were shattered, while the industrialized states benefited, initially from the gains of monopoly capitalism and overseas investment, and eventually under the auspices of finance capital. Over the centuries the world shrank gradually; it became integrated, albeit in an asymmetrical fashion by which vast regions of the globe served the interests of the few industrialized states. Even at the end of World War II, despite a postcolonial era during which sovereign and legally equal states became the accepted international norm, the economic dependence of the non Western world, which the West itself had created, persisted. Furthermore, though no longer under colonial rule, during the Cold War era most non industrialized countries became political clients of the United States or the Soviet Union.

Globalization thus was in formation for centuries. Its distinctive feature in recent decades, however, has been the contraction of time and space enabling split-second financial and communications transactions throughout the world. A global economy has come into existence that transcends the state, changing the latter's role and function and/or diminishing state sovereignty in many realms. Contemporary globalization is multifaceted. A global consumer market and its attendant uniform product distribution is destroying the diverse unique handicrafts, attire, architecture, visual and performing arts, and even foods of different cultures and societies. Standardization and uniformity are replacing distinctiveness and versatility. Mergers and acquisitions at both the domestic level and across borders are everyday events, while the productive facilities of multinationals are spread throughout the world in the search for cheap labour, which often includes child labor, and the appropriate investment climate. Financial transactions, including currency speculation, are instantaneous. Moreover, modern technology in turn enables communication, information, and knowledge to be transmitted rapidly, at least to those who are privileged enough to have access to computers, e-mail, and the Internet.

Appreciating the Scope of Globalization

Above all, globalization refers to the emergence of a world economy in which international financial transactions; stock, bond, and futures market exchanges; and currency mobility are supplemented by a worldwide labor market and global production facilities. The integration of politics, technology, information, and capital has created a global marketplace that is "characterized not just by global free trade but more specifically by the free movement of capital." As market forces command free trade and competition, it is alleged that the economy becomes more transparent and, therefore, "the more efficient and flourishing the economy will be. " Dominated by multinationals based in the United States (whose authority, at least for the time being, remains unchallenged by any countervailing state power), the globalized economy is buttressed by the ascendency of the technological forces unleashed by the corporate giants IBM, Microsoft, Intel, and Cisco Systems, among others. The hardware, software, microprocessors, and Internet routers created by these corporate giants, along with digitization, fiber optics, and satellite communications, allow for instantaneous financial activity.

The system can be envisaged as a gigantic circulatory system, sucking capital into the financial markets and institutions at the center and then pumping it out to the periphery.

In the year 1996 alone, $93 billion poured into Indonesia, Malaysia, the Philippines, South Korea, and Thailand. In 1997, as the Asian economic crisis erupted, the net outflow from the five countries was $12 billion. The almost instantaneous withdrawal of Western investment, and the ensuing crisis, led the International Monetary Fund (IMF) to insist on its long-standing structural adjustment policy (also commonly applied to Africa), which caused currencies to be devalued and prices to rise, while real wages and employment plummeted. Exports tumbled or remained stagnant, and current account deficits rose. According to Ruth Heifer, former chairperson of the Federal Deposit Insurance Corporation, "Financial liberalization was undertaken in countries that didn't have the infrastructure to support it. That was one of the principal causes of the Asian crisis," which was compounded by bad and over-extended loans. As the emergency widened, reaching Latin America and Russia, economies collapsed and political and social turmoil spread. Between June 1997 and December 1998, as primarily Western investors rapidly withdrew their capital, values on the Russian stockmarket declined 86 percent, while in Indonesia stocks fell 80 percent, in the Philippines 54 percent, Thailand 42 percent, Malaysia 74 percent, and South Korea 29 percent. During the same period, Germany's stock market rose 54 percent, while that in the United States increased by 31 percent.

Investors and state actors in charge of directing flows of capital have created in this new world of technological globalization what Hans-Peter Martin and Harald Schumann refer to as "the right of money to vote." "It is not a question of morality fund managers are only carrying out instructions by seeking the highest possible return on capital but their superior power now allows them to challenge every step forward in social equality that has been painfully achieved."

Buttressed by the neoliberal principles of open borders and free markets (whose leading advocate is Milton Friedman), most states pursue, or are forced to capitulate to, liberalization policies dictated by the flows of capital while the IMF and the World Bank impose the policies as conditions for loans to debt-ridden countries. Moreover, as a result of the North American Free Trade Agreement, U. S. multinationals can easily shift production facilities to places like Mexico, ignoring labor rights and reasonable wages. The World Trade Organization attempts to impose free trade on a worldwide scale. The era of import substitution policies as the strategy for development by underdeveloped countries has ended. Overall, global actors international finance and multinationals are not accountable to the state for their actions even though they affect hundreds of millions of people. Quite the opposite, states are now accountable to this private economic regime. Indeed, it is estimated that as a result of the economic crisis that struck Indonesia and the structural adjustment program imposed by the IMF more than 100 million people there are now living below the poverty line.

It should be noted that centralized administrative headquarters for multinationals are mostly located in the financial capitals of the highly industrialized states. The latter in turn have become the foremost advocates of globalization. Meanwhile, the end of the Cold War has resulted in a significant decline in aid for development purposes by industrialized states. Africa, which during the Cold War era received massive military and economic aid, has not been incorporated into the global economy (except for the Republic of South Africa), and in fact has seen the virtual demise of several of its states such as Somalia, Sierra Leone, and Zaire (now the Democratic Republic of Congo). During the last days of 1999, even the once-stable Ivory Coast saw its civilian government overthrown by the military.

The proponents of neoliberalism, to morally justify globalization, or what George Soros refers to as "free market fundamentalism," wrap their philosophy in the mantle of the universalist position on human rights. According to Kenneth Anderson, formerly of Human Rights Watch:

As the global market economy pulverized traditional societies and moralities and drew every corner of the planet into a single economic machine, human rights emerged as the secular creed that the new global middle class needed in order to justify their domination of the new cosmopolitan order.

But it is highly questionable whether human rights, certainly from the perspective of economic and social rights, but even so far as the power of the vote is concerned, are reinforced by globalization. According to the World Bank, the heart of the Asian crisis was "the surge of capital flows." Blaming global investors, and Asian officials and entrepreneurs eager to obtain investment capital, the World Bank maintained that "the surge in is followed by a precipitous flow out." The policies implemented by the IMF "spread the economic pain far beyond the banks, investment funds and real estate companies that got the countries into trouble to begin with, sending thousands of small businesses into bankruptcy. Some estimates are that levels of bankruptcy in Indonesia now are 75 percent. " And the International Labour Organization, in its report on the Asian events, predicted that as many of these nations begin to "recover" from economic catastrophe, unemployment in South Korea will increase to 8.2 from 2.3 percent, while 12 percent of South Koreans will fall below the poverty line.

Meanwhile, Japan, one of the Group of 7 (the highly industrialized states), has been experiencing economic decline leading to unheard of levels of unemployment and homelessness.

Global integration, what Edward Luttwak refers to as "turbo-capitalism," has become a dictatorship of the world market and appears unstoppable. But, for "many hundreds of millions, globalized progress is no progress at all." United Nations Secretary General Kofi Annan, speaking before the elite of world corporate and political power at the 1999 World Economic Forum at Davos, Switzerland, reflected on the downside of the open global marketplace, and in so doing echoed third world vulnerability to its demands.

We have to choose between a global market driven only by calculations of short-term profit and one which has a human face. You can at least make sure that you yourselves are not employing underage children to forced labor, either directly or indirectly. The spread of markets far outpaces the abilities of societies and their political systems to adjust to them. Globalization is a fact of life. But I believe we have underestimated its fragility.

Globalization can be seen as an extension of the U. S. policy of Manifest Destiny; the capitalist equivalent of the Monroe Doctrine. And in terms of human rights, it is often argued, globalization has assisted in their diffusion and reinforced the Western concept of universalism "since markets break down traditional social structures and encourage the emergence of assertive temperaments." Thus the financial marketplace, U. S. foreign policy, and human rights are all interrelated, increasing the already enormous power of the United States in insinuating its authority and leverage worldwide. Or, as Thomas Friedman so inelegantly put it in his paean to globalization, "as a jogger in this world you will be run over by a Formula One car."

State sovereignty, as historically understood since the Peace of Westphalia, is being undermined. Although state sovereignty was never absolute, the constraints were self-imposed as a result of bilateral or multilateral treaties or, on occasion, customary law. The changing role of the state nowadays is embodied in policies of liberalization and deregulation, thus becoming a facilitator of globalization. Of great significance is the fact that even in democratic states the citizenry is excluded from participation in decisions, policies, or actions taken by global actors that directly affect citizens' daily lives and welfare. The stock and bond markets, rather than the voting booth, have become the preeminent mediators of the globalization debate. Furthermore, despite fierce competitiveness among multinational corporations and financiers, at least at present, international regulatory agencies of the global economy comparable to those at the domestic level do not exist, leaving financial actors and multinationals to devise their own norms and their own regime.

Neoliberalism, with its doctrine of open borders and free markets, represents policies that are pursued by the overwhelming majority of states, either voluntarily or as imposed by the IMF and the World Bank. Globalization is devoid of ideological or humanistic underpinnings, although, as Soros maintains, its free-market ideology is evident. It is a contemporary sterile version of John Locke's conceptualization of man in pursuit of his material self-interest and of Adam Smith's invisible hand that denotes the power of the market. It certainly does not have its premise in the utilitarians' belief in the greatest good for the greatest number. Thus, neoliberalism has accelerated the emergence of a new global capitalist class whose loyalty is to profits and wealth, not to any nation-state. The God of the neoliberals is wealth and its continual accumulation. Concurrently, the "marginals, " as David Apter labels those who have failed to participate in or been excluded from the development process, do not benefit from the modern global economy.

Studies of globalization have proliferated in the past several years. Few, however, address in depth the simultaneous process of fragmentation at the local level and, in particular, the linkages between these two superficially contradictory processes. Many more analyses do confront the negative consequences of globalization, namely the marginalization of millions of people who are nonproductive in the global economy. A reaction to globalization has occurred due to an intensification of turmoil and conflict, labor strife, and increased ethnic, racial, and religious tensions. In fact, Kofi Annan, in his 1999 address to the World Economic Forum, addressed just this point. He maintained that until people build confidence in "the global economy," it will be fragile and vulnerable vulnerable to backlash from all the "isms" of our post-cold-war world: protectionism, populism, nationalism, ethnic chauvinism, fanaticism and terrorism.

It is vital at this point in history, as the world moves into the new millennium, to investigate to what extent the insecurity and anomie of contemporary life that have accompanied the collapse of overarching ideologies, the attendant sense of loss of control over one's individual or communal identity and destiny, and the current stymying of the liberating spirit of the Enlightenment have fuelled these conflicts in the search for a new belonging and new meanings.

Prosperity for Whom

Human rights have been on the international agenda since the end of World War II, certainly since 1948, but their violation as a consequence of globalization has not been adequately examined. The "international bill of human rights" holds states accountable for implementation of human rights. But in the contemporary era it is the private global actors that are frequently the most egregious violators of rights, and as stated earlier they are accountable to no one and to no institution or state. Although data on human rights violations exist, in-depth analysis is needed to substantiate the deleterious effects of globalization on economic and social rights, including labor rights. Strikes and demonstrations protesting worsening labor conditions have become widespread, including in communally based societies where individual political action has been rare. Political authorities often react to this strife by increasing restrictions on civil and political rights and, at times, grossly violating basic rights, such as the right to life, in an effort to control the labor force. Human rights NGOs have extensively documented thc increase in labour activism, particularly in such low-wage areas as Malaysia, Indonesia, and even China, and the concomitant increase in state repression.

In addition to labor strife, globalization has resulted in the intensification of ethnic and religious conflict and violence. Globalization with its attendant social change has precipitated fragmentation at the local level. On the one hand, the resurgence of ethnic and religious strife can be understood as an effort to assert identities and to ascribe meaning in the face of global forces over which one has no control. However there is another dimension to ethnic/religious strife that needs to be scrutinized. What is a particular ethnicity's class position both within the state and globally? It may be that ethnic/religious and class categories overlap. It is well known, for example, that in Indonesia, where ethnic strife has erupted, the majority of merchants and retailers are Chinese. In such cases, a critical issue is raised as to whether, analytically, ethnic/religious clashes or class conflict is the decisive factor in increased violence.

With the end of the Cold War, Africa, excluding the Republic of South Africa, lost its geopolitical importance. Subsequently, despite some major French investments in Gabon and the Ivory Coast, British financing in Kenya, and Shell Oil's facilities in eastern Nigeria, the continent has on the whole been marginalized and has not been incorporated into the global economy. Shell Oil periodically faces worker protests and demonstrations by ethnic and environmental groups. Such outbreaks have been fiercely repressed by the Nigerian government. Politically many states, such as Burundi, Rwanda, Somalia, and Liberia, have disintegrated, and violence has erupted along clan and/or ethnic lines. Not only has economic development failed to materialize, but the imposition, particularly in the past few decades, of the IMF's structural adjustment programs has resulted (for example, in Ghana) in declining wages, increased unemployment, poverty, and a precipitous decline in social services, including funding for education.

Furthermore, human rights violations (whether of individual civil/political, economic/social, or minority rights) as a consequence of destructive social change resulting from globalization might result, at least in some instances, in radical shifts in a society's cultural values and norms that, in turn, may lead to a reconfiguration of the substance of traditional or historic notions of human rights. The outcome of this search for a revitalized identity and meaning is unpredictable. There may be a reinforcement of an exclusive communalism with little personal autonomy or there may be a loosening of communal ties and an expansion of individual demands based on class. The evidence points in both directions. Clearly globalization has had a deleterious effect on the entire complex of human rights, resulting in significant transformations in the behavior and values of masses of humanity across the globe. Further research is vital if the ramifications of globalization on ethnicity, class, and religion, and on the interrelationship among them, are to be fully comprehended.

The negative shock of globalization has, it should be noted, affected not only non-Western societies, but those of advanced, industrialized Western Europe, the United States, and Japan. The consequences of globalization for the poor and middle class in the United States are enormous. "The wealthiest and most productive country in the world has changed into the largest low-wage economy. In 1995 four-fifths of all male employees and workers in the United States earned 11 percent less an hour in real terms than they did in 1973. " According to Kevin Phillips, "Caste and class restraints that had eased after World War II began to reemerge" in the 1980s, and by 1995 the Federal Reserve Bank had found that in 1989 the wealthiest 1 percent of American households with a net worth of at least $2.3 million each owned nearly 40 percent of the nation's wealth, and the top 20 percent of Americans households worth $180,000 or more owned more than 80 percent of the country's wealth. By 1999, according to the Congressional Budget Office, the wealthiest 2.7 million Americans had as much to spend as the poorest 100 million, while income disparity had grown so much that four out of five households took home a thinner slice of the economic pie than they did in 1977. At the end of the century the gap between rich and poor Americans has turned into a chasm. As astounding capital accumulation was occurring in the upper tier of U. S. society, between 1977 and 1999 the average family income of the middle class fell by 3.1 percent, while that of the poorest income decile dropped a startling 12.0 percent. During the same period, family income of the highest decile rose by a whopping 119.7 percent. Even in Germany the dismantling of the welfare state can be discerned, despite the fact that its social inequality is not as profound as in the United States, while the traditional eastern German culture that had survived even during communist rule is now being globalized and overrun with western German capital and values.

Although the United States is a society based on individualism, and does not view economic and social rights as fundamental, from Franklin Roosevelt's New Deal to Lyndon Johnson's Great Society it had taken on many of the attributes of a welfare state. But, under Ronald Reagan, George Bush, and Bill Clinton many of the structures of the welfare state have been dismantled. At the same time privatization of industry *and* of social services has become a guiding principle of government policy. As a consequence of the restructuring of corporations, downsizing, outsourcing, use of contract labour, and movement of production facilities to cheap-labour countries, matched with record profits for corporations, the well-being of ordinary citizens has deteriorated. In April 2000, the United States lauded itself for a continuing decline in the unemployment rate to 4.2 percent of the workforce. This figure is deceptive because, in contrast to the method that Germany, for example, uses to measure unemployment, only those actively looking for work are included, while part-time workers are considered employed regardless of their income. Furthermore, much of the increase in employment is in the low-skill, low-paying service sector, which does little to bring employees into the middle class or to keep them there. The relatively new corporate policy of hiring contract labor does not provide for fringe benefits. Neoliberal policies, which include privatization of public services, have in turn resulted in a decline in education expenditures, cutbacks in health services, and severe reductions in aid for the destitute and the unemployed.

Nothing reveals the consequences of globalization in the United States more dramatically than the widening income gap between the wealthiest and the poorest, and the collapse of much of its rural economy "as a result of the global wage differentials of the 1980s. Cheap, willing, rural non-union American labour was no longer cheap enough," and consequently rural poverty has been increasing at twice the rate of urban poverty. Globalization's impact in and on the United States is not nearly as generous to all its citizens as its supporters make it out to be.

Human Rights: Globalization and the Future

Clearly globalization can, insofar as its deleterious effects are concerned, be likened to a new version of colonialism and imperialism. Throughout the past decade industrial states have facilitated largely Western financial institutions, investment banks, and formidable corporations in accumulating an enormous amount of capital and power that they have used to deeply penetrate exogenous societies. As Michael Davis has indicated,

> *Many communities in East Asia have experienced problems with labor rights abuse and massive worker displacement. Global intrusion has often been accompanied by increased problems with unemployment, crime, corruption and environmental degradation.*

The inherent principle of globalization is to develop economic transparency so as to improve the efficiencies of economies worldwide for the benefit of the industrial powers and non-Western states. But an underlying, equally important assumption is that civil and political rights must be raised above economic and social rights so as to buttress economic growth and development. Since political rights are seen as intrinsically correlative with the growth of an economy, the latter is seen as impossible to accomplish without the former. Philosophically speaking, the concepts of John Locke and Adam Smith must operate in tandem to create a free and unfettered economy.

As a result, under the rubric of globalization non-Western nations are pressured to accept neoliberal principles of free trade and open markets and the universalist concept of human rights. They are given little choice, irrespective of the economic dislocations or political havoc that may result. Even a power such as China has embarked on economic liberalization with the encouragement of foreign investors who establish production facilities with low-wage labor. Weaker and more marginal states, such as Kenya, Ethiopia, and Indonesia, are less able to successfully stave off such pressure. Cuba, which is hardly a threat any longer to U. S. national interests, remains in the vise of the 40-year-old embargo because it refuses to accept U. S. demands to alter its political and economic systems, accepting the principle of political and civil rights and jettisoning its belief system based on the paramountcy of economic rights. Counter to the prevailing norm, Prime Minister Mahathir Mohamad of Malaysia in September 1998 responded to the financial crisis by reasserting state sovereignty in economic policy; he closed the borders and imposed currency controls.

The United States in the twenty-first century is more powerful and dominant than any nation or empire has ever been, and it has become a handmaiden to corporate and financial interests. No state can match it in military prowess, and none can, at least for very long, constrain its demands. The United States can rescue Mexico from economic collapse, as it did in 1995, when Secretary of the Treasury Robert Rubin amazingly took virtual control of Mexico's economy to save it and U.S. investors from the destructiveness of the globalized international money market regime. It can create the conditions for malnutrition and a destroyed health care system in Cuba to force the country to bow to U. S. demands for the acceptance of a universal human rights program. In Thailand, Indonesia, and South Korea, it worked together with the IMF to effect structural adjustment policies, while, in a successful attempt to keep Boris Yeltsin in power, it watched billions of dollars in aid to Russia disappear into the hands of a corrupt elite that siphoned off the funds to banks in Cyprus, Switzerland, and elsewhere, while the Russian population sank deeper into poverty and despair. In 1998, the United States bombed and destroyed a Sudanese pharmaceutical plant because it was suspected, erroneously, that the facility was part of a terrorist network supported by the Saudi Arabian militant suspected of masterminding the bombings of U. S. embassies in Kenya and Tanzania. And in 1999, together with its NATO allies, it led a 78-day bombing campaign against Serbia to halt Yugoslavian President Slobodan Milosevic's vicious ethnic cleansing campaign in Kosovo. Militarily, economically, and politically the United States is the twenty-first-century colossus that all nations must contend with, and that many turn to.

If the destructive economic and political effects of globalization are to be ameliorated, both the industrial states and their clients and adversaries are going to have to stifle their dogmatism. The United States, in its pursuit of a globalized world, should accept the premise that cultural differences political, social, and economic must be more than merely tolerated, but must be incorporated into a new framework of globalization. Economic dislocations, ethnic violence, labor unrest, and religious conflict will never be completely eliminated but can be reduced by compromise. Simply because the United States is as powerful as it is does not give it a monopoly on knowledge, accuracy, or sensitivity. Nor do the values embedded in the "ideology" of multinationals and financiers address the needs and values of much of humanity. At the same time, non-Western states that continue to engage in severe economic and political repression are going to have to alter their despotic ways; not because the United States will demand it, but because it is morally right to be responsive to the demands of their people, and it will create the conditions for the integration of their populations into a more democratic and legitimate political order. After all, the rondas in northern Peru exist largely because the state judicial system is seen as corrupt, tyrannical, and often nonfunctional.

The precepts of globalization must be modified to incorporate human rights. Furthermore, an integration of the principles of cultural relativists and universalists should take place, which would lead to a less strident, less destructive globalism. The global information highway can facilitate this process. The United States, as a world power, first and foremost should accept the principle of diversity in the arena of human rights. How the integration of apparently diverse and dissimilar philosophies can be accomplished in the context of globalization requires further research and analysis.

Bibliography

Akermark, Athanasia Spiliopoulou (1997) Justifications of Minority Protection in International Law. London, The Hague, and Boston: Kluwer Law International.

Bauer, Joanne R. and Daniel A. Bell, eds. (1999) The East Asian Challenge for Human Rights. Cambridge: Cambridge University Press.

Cassese, Antonio (1991) Human Rights in a Changing World. Philadelphia: Temple University Press.

Davis, Michael C., ed. (1995) Human Rights and Chinese Values: Legal, Philosophical and Political Perspectives. Oxford and New York: Oxford University Press.

Falk, Richard A. (2000) Human Rights Horizons: The Pursuit of Justice in a Globalizing World. New York and London: Routledge.

Guilhot, Nicolas. *The Democracy Makers: Human Rights and the Politics of Global Order.* New York: Columbia University Press, 2005.

Gustafson, Carie and Peter Juviler, eds. (1998) Religion and Human Rights: Competing Claims? New York: M.E. Sharpe.

Hannum, Hurst (1990) Autonomy, Sovereignty, and Self - Determination: The Accommodation of Conflicting Rights. Philadelphia: University of Pennsylvania Press.

Jacobson, David ((1997) Rights Across Borders: Immigration and the Decline of Citizenship. Baltimore and London: The Johns Hopkins University Press.

Kimlycka, Will, ed. (1995) The Rights of Minority Cultures. Oxford and New York: Oxford University Press.

Lauren, Paul Gordon (1998) The Evolution of International Human Rights: Visions Seen. Philadelphia: University of Pennsylvania Press.

Mayer, Ann E. (1999) Islam and Human Rights: Tradition and Politics. Oxford and Boulder: Westview Press.

Musgrave, Thomas D. (1997) Self-Determination and National Minorities. Oxford: Clarendon Press.

Ojo, Bamidele A. (1997) Human Rights and the New World Order: Universality, Acceptability, and Human Diversity. Commack, New York: Nova Science Publishers.

Risse, Thomas, Stephen C. Ropp, and Kathryn Sikkink, eds. (1999) The Power of Human Rights: International Norms and Domestic Change. Cambridge: Cambridge University Press.

Rowe, Peter. *The Impact of Human Rights Law on Armed Forces.* Cambridge, UK: Cambridge University Press, 2006.

Spinner-Halev, Jeff (1994) The Boundaries of Citizenship: Race, Ethnicity, and Nationality in the Liberal State. Baltimore: Johns Hopkins University Press.

Tolley, Howard B., Jr. *The International Commission of Jurists: Global Advocates for Human Rights.* Philadelphia, PA: University of Pennsylvania Press, 1994.

Van Dyke, Vernon (1985) Human Rights, Ethnicity, and Discrimination. Westport, Connecticut: Greenwood Press.

Welch, Claude E., Jr. and Virginia A. Leary, eds. (1990) Asian Perspectives on Human Rights. Boulder, Colorado: Westview Press.

Index

Universal Jurisdiction, 19